Dear Country Music Fans:

You are some of the best people in the world. Your love of music, your big hearts, and your devotion to the artists make the music possible. Without you, the only packed house a musical genius like Vince Gill would be playing to would be his own. Because of you, he kept on playing for the many years when he was a musical genius but not a musical star. I hope you love reading about Vince's journey to the top as much as I loved writing about it.

Thanks to you fans, I've had the opportunity to write about the lives and the music of LeAnn Rimes, George Strait, and Brooks & Dunn in addition to Vince. I've had more fun than you can imagine. To everyone who has read my books, to all of you I've met at Fan Fair, and to all the listeners of the country music radio stations who kindly invited me to be on the air—a big hearty thank-you.

Let's keep celebrating America's own great music—let's keep celeb

By Jo Sgammato
Published by Ballantine Books:

DREAM COME TRUE: *The LeAnn Rimes Story*
KEEPIN' IT COUNTRY: *The George Strait Story*
COUNTRY'S GREATEST DUO: *The Brooks & Dunn Story*
FOR THE MUSIC: *The Vince Gill Story*

FOR THE MUSIC

The Vince Gill Story

Jo Sgammato

BALLANTINE BOOKS • NEW YORK

A Ballantine Book
Published by The Ballantine Publishing Group
Copyright © 1999 by Jo Sgammato

All rights reserved under International and Pan-American Copyright Conventions. Published in the United States by The Ballantine Publishing Group, a division of Random House, Inc., New York, and simultaneously in Canada by Random House of Canada Limited, Toronto.

Ballantine and colophon are registered trademarks of Random House, Inc.

Cover photo © Mark Humphrey/AP/Wide World Photos

www.randomhouse.com/BB/

Library of Congress Catalog Card Number: 99-90028

ISBN 0-345-43106-5

Manufactured in the United States of America

First Edition: April 1999

10 9 8 7 6 5 4 3 2 1

For Ira Fraitag—
for the music

and

for Laurie Dean Kraman—
for the harmony

Contents

Contents

CHAPTER ONE

Nicest Guy in Nashville

"As you see me now, that's the way I'll be ten years from now; the way I was ten years ago."
—VINCE GILL

That's exactly what we love about him.

While many superstar artists go to great lengths to cultivate and project a "regular guy" image, Vince Gill wouldn't even know how to do that. He's too real, too regular, too much the guy next door to ever think of pretending to be anything other than what he is.

What is he? An extraordinarily talented and creative artist with a gift for every aspect of music making. Let's start with what listeners first notice—a pure tenor voice with perfect pitch. It's the sound equivalent of sheer silk, rich velvet, a midnight blue sky filled with stars. No one else can wring so much emotion from the notes of a song and make it appear so effortless. Like the greatest singers of every kind of music who have come before him—like Frank Sinatra, Tony Bennett, George Jones, Hank Williams—Vince Gill is a true original who can bring the sounds of any song to a whole new level, touching our hearts as he seems to be completely revealing his

1

own. In a world where so many singers are indistinguishable from one another, Vince's voice and style are immediately recognized with just a few notes.

Yet, amazingly, for many years he didn't consider himself a singer at all. "I've always thought of myself as a guitar player who could sing," he said. In fact, as recently as 1996, he told a reporter that he'd once been afraid to sing.

> "I was a guitarist first but only because I was too shy to sing. That's why I keep my eyes closed when I sing—I'm afraid to look."
>
> —VINCE GILL

Well, eyes open or closed, Vince Gill is the ultimate singer. That voice has not only made him a major star in his own right, it keeps him in high demand as a background vocalist for dozens of other artists.

But he's also a great guitar player, one of the best of our times. Many fans don't realize until they see him in concert that Vince Gill plays his own lead guitar, a rarity among singers, particularly in the country music field. Critics have called him one of the best guitarists of his generation, whose guitar playing rings closer to rock and roll than traditional or modern country. His guitar solos are seamless continuations of the lyrics of his songs, played as only a singer would play them. Guitar aficionados compare him to, among others, blues and rock superstar Eric Clapton for tone, feeling, and tastefulness. Vince is a big fan of country guitarist extraordinaire Chet Atkins and, as one reviewer said, "every bit the quiet guitar man's musical equal." But don't look to Vince to acknowledge how great his guitar playing is. All he'll say about it is, "I'm a pretty decent rock guitar player, but my true gift is honestly pickin' and singin'."

As if all that weren't enough, Vince Gill is an amazing and accomplished songwriter. Much has been made of the singer/songwriter in the field of pop music, but it is rare that a country superstar writes his or her own songs. Instead, most rely on the wonderful community of talented songwriters in Nashville and beyond to provide the songs that showcase their voices. Vince is an exception to that rule. He has written or co-written almost all the songs he has ever recorded. His success as a singer/songwriter within country music may be one reason so many pop singer/songwriters have come to Nashville, where they can display their talents to a country audience that has more appreciation for the song itself.

In 1990, one song catapulted Vince Gill to the top stratosphere of country music after many years in many kinds of music. It was the eloquent and heart wrenching "When I Call Your Name," which he co-wrote with another music business giant, college professor turned record company president Tim DuBois.

Since then, Vince Gill has written many top-notch songs that range from the most traditional country standards to pop-influenced ballads, from country-rock classics to pure bluegrass and blues. His lyrics can be heartbreakingly sad or filled with fun and wit. But they always reflect that mysterious and awesome songwriting talent—great economy of words—finding just the right turn of phrase to capture and communicate a universal feeling in a new and remarkable way.

Nashville, Tennessee, where Vince Gill has lived for

the past fifteen years, can accurately boast that the best
songwriters in the business call it home—from classic
country songsmiths like Harlan Howard, Whitey Shafer,
Hank Cochran, and Dean Dillon to today's hit makers like
Tony Arata, Pat Alger, Dave Loggins, and Keith Hinton.
Even writers from other musical genres—people like Michael McDonald, formerly of the Doobie Brothers, disco
diva Donna Summer, and pop masters like Neil Diamond
and Bert Bacharach—have either moved to Nashville or
spend lots of time there writing new songs. Nashville is to
country music what Tin Pan Alley once was to Broadway.

> "Living here and being part of a community
> driven by songwriters makes you feel great to
> be considered one of them."
>
> —VINCE GILL

Once, while accepting a songwriting honor in Nashville,
Vince shared his love for his adopted hometown with a national television audience. "The songwriting community
of this town is its lifeblood," he said, "and it always will be
when all is said and done. To be among you as a songwriter is a great thrill."

From the beginning, fans, critics, journalists, and music
industry insiders have seen Vince Gill for exactly what he
is—a triple threat. Beautiful singer. Amazing guitarist.
Accomplished songwriter. Vince Gill is always humble
when he hears others sing his praises. He hasn't worked
all these years for the money, the acclaim, the gold and
platinum album sales, or the sold-out concert tours. He
hasn't even done it for all the awards—and there are
dozens—that fill his shelves. It's the songs he's created

and the people he's met that are his most treasured mementos. From the lean years to the superstar years, Vince Gill has always worked hard and played beautifully, toured extensively and recorded with style and class, for one thing only, for the music.

"I still do it because I love playing," he said. "Whether I'd become famous never mattered because I love playing so much."

That love is evident. It's what has garnered Vince so many fans of all ages, from grandparents to their grandchildren.

Men love Vince Gill because he's such a regular guy. Women love him for that, too, and for the fact that, as one reporter said, the general consensus among the ladies is that Vince is a "hunk-a-rama." Or as Jim West, program manager of KAT Country Radio in Albuquerque, New Mexico, put it, "He's got those movie star good looks."

MCA Records' Tony Brown, a veteran musician, record producer, and music industry leader, played in a band with Vince Gill in the 1980s and produced his megaselling albums in the 1990s. He says Vince Gill is like a gunslinger.

> "He can fire off a hit song, he looks like a million bucks, and he can play as good as any session player in town. I think musically and vocally he can do anything he wants."
> —TONY BROWN

From lovers of pop to hard-core country traditionalists, from producers and engineers of hard-rock music to songwriters in general, everyone who loves music loves Vince

Gill. His sheer talent, honesty, and love for his craft are what take center stage.

And it isn't just the fans who have made Vince one of the most beloved country artists of his time—or any time. Everyone in the industry regards him with the highest love and respect. The one and only Garth Brooks has often said, "I just wish I could sing like Vince Gill."

Many of the fans who have loved Vince Gill throughout the 1990s may not know that he's been a working musician since he was in his teens. His boyish good looks and youthful approach to life make it hard to believe that he's been in the music business for more than twenty years. He's too modest to boast about everything he's done—he's been a sideman, a studio backup singer, a session guitarist, a songwriter, a band leader, and a multi-platinum recording artist. He has sung backup for numerous artists on some of the major albums of our time. And now that he's a big star, the best singers and musicians jump at the chance to sing and play with him on his own records as well as on the many collaborative record projects he participates in. He's performed everywhere from beer joints and honky tonks to bluegrass festivals and country dance halls, from ornate music halls backed by symphony orchestras to outdoor concert stages with a rock band. When he celebrated two decades as a working musician, he remarked, "I didn't look at it as achieving a goal. I just enjoy singing and playing and I still feel about music like I did when I was eighteen."

So many people dream of a career in music. Many have the talent, some have the drive, a few even have the good luck to make it. One of the things that usually gets in the way is the need to make a living. Earning money isn't always easy when you're pursuing a dream.

Vince Gill's abilities as a guitarist, studio musician, and background singer kept him working long before his solo career took off. They helped him to hone his skills and to be involved in doing what he loved the most.

About his long road to success, he says, "The timing of things wasn't always right for me. It took a long time, but in hindsight, it gave me a lot of time to watch and learn a lot of things.

"The thing I'm proudest of is that I've always had the ability to make a living musically," he says, adding, "It wasn't always a lot of money."

He always had the talent, but it took a while to make it big. They say in Nashville that a lot of people may have talent, but it's those with the most persistence who are successful. Vince was persistent, patient, and always kept his sense of humor. Even during the lean years, he was guided by the belief that he would attain, both in life and in music, whatever he was supposed to get. "And that's fine," he said.

Ultimately, what makes Vince Gill a great artist is that he does it all for the music. He knows that honest emotion and a clear, focused voice will bring the listeners to him. Nowhere is this more evident than on his latest album, *The Key*.

"The most inspiring mainstream country album to come out in 1998 even with the Christmas superstar releases still ahead."
—Associated Press

In June 1998, listeners to country music radio stations were swooning. Amid all the familiar hits they'd been listening to for months came a new single by Vince Gill that, quite simply, blew them away. Here was one of the richest voices of l990s country music singing a song that sounded like it came straight out of country's deepest and oldest roots, with a twist of 1960s soul thrown in for good measure. Where had Vince found this great song? Well, he had just written it.

"If You Ever Have Forever in Mind" was the first single from Vince Gill's first new album in two years, *The Key*, slated to be released a few months later. Backed by a wonderful, lush string section and dreamy harmony vocals, Vince Gill was singing a song that thrilled the emotions of anyone who loves love and dazzled the musical sensibilities of everyone who appreciates a truly great song. With all of its flourishes and richness, it was still a thoroughly country ballad, delivered with the utmost style.

The song really did have a 1960s Nashville sound. Vince wrote it with Tony Seals and it featured background vocals by Dennis William Wilson, Lisa Silver, Marabeth Jordan, John Mark Ivey, Lisa Cochran, and Michael Eldred. It was inspired by the songs and style of a very special album by another musical giant. *Modern Sounds in Country and Western Music* by Ray Charles, released thirty-seven years ago, was the lightning bolt that liberated country music. You could even make the case that it was the lesson of that album that allowed an artist like Vince Gill to make it big in Nashville. So let's pause in our story to spend a little time with Ray Charles.

Even back in 1962, music was being categorized as to the kind of sound it had and the kind of audience it was looking to appeal to. Ray Charles had quite a reputation as a master of rhythm and blues among black music fans, but white audiences, accustomed to what was called more mainstream music, had yet to fully discover him. At the time, neither black audiences nor urban white audiences were listening much to country.

The president of Charles's record label, ABC-Paramount Records, at that time was Sam Clark. When Ray Charles first proposed doing an album of country music, Clark warned him that he might lose some of the fans he had gained while building his reputation in r&b. As a real music man, Ray Charles replied that even though he might lose some old fans, he might just as easily gain some new ones if he played the songs as well as he felt he could. Years later, the incomparable singer admitted he was bluffing when he'd said that. "I didn't know what I was talking about," Charles said, laughing. "But I wanted to do it, so that's what I said to him."

"Charles understood country music," said Sid Feller, then ABC-Paramount's A&R (artist and repertoire) director. "He loved the simple and plaintive lyrics and wanted to give country a new approach. He felt that by giving the music a lush treatment, it could be different from what country singers would do with the material."

Ray Charles had very definite ideas about the arrangements of the songs on the albums. There were lush strings, fabulous saxophone solos, and the great sound of Ray Charles's big band. He created an album as different from the country music of the time as he had intended. When it came to doing his part, Ray played piano and sang "live" with the musicians. The songs were selected from the greatest country hits of the previous ten to fifteen years. Hank Williams hits that got a new spin from Ray Charles were "Half as Much," "You Win Again," and "Hey, Good Lookin'." The Everly Brothers' first hit, 1957's "Bye Bye Love," led off the album. Floyd Tillman's 1939 hit "It Makes No Difference Now" was the album's oldest song.

Four of the songs were released as singles. "I Can't Stop Loving You" stayed on *Billboard*'s pop chart at number one for five weeks and became a signature song for Ray Charles. The other three—"Careless Love," "Born to Lose," and "You Don't Know Me"—also charted on *Billboard*'s pop chart. The album itself remained on *Billboard*'s pop album chart for nearly two years and spent an amazing fourteen weeks in the number-one position.

Modern Sounds in Country and Western Music opened country music to a much wider audience than it had in the 1960s. It made record companies and producers more comfortable with trying new approaches and trusting the instincts of the artists. Most significantly, the album woke Nashville up to the notion that music didn't have to be so strictly forced into categories—a lesson the business has been learning ever since. With "If You Ever Have Forever in Mind," Vince Gill honored that classic album and joined the ranks of tremendous talents who don't worry about categories or the classifications of songs and sounds, artists who follow their hearts for the music.

> "You've gotta have an open mind about music. Over the years, my greatest asset has been my ears. If I didn't hear the different sounds, I wouldn't be able to make them on my records."
> —VINCE GILL

Like all great musical artists, Vince doesn't restrict himself to listening to only one kind of music. His tastes range wide and he bemoans the narrow formatting of music that is the result of so many different radio stations trying to appeal to what they would call "segments of the market."

"It would be very sad if we started taking country music and pushing it into that young-country format where they don't play anything prior to 1990," he says. "Country needs to look at musical styles for what they are. If it leans toward rock, play it for what it's supposed to be. If it's r&b, show some respect and play it. Don't water it down to fit some format."

As a musician's musician, Gill obviously shares the belief of real music lovers that there are truly only two kinds of music—good music and bad music. "It's the music that's important," he says, "and if the music is good, it doesn't matter who's playing it." And as a guitarist, he is completely unrestricted in his tastes. Whether it's Eric Clapton playing "Layla" or Chet Atkins performing "Freight Train," Vince finds them "equally brilliant. I've always loved great singer/guitar players. The type of music didn't matter as long as you could find some sort of incredible guitar solo."

Having mastered so many kinds of music himself, Vince Gill created with *The Key* his most traditional country music album ever. He didn't do it for any kind of "marketing" reasons. It was just where he was as an artist at the time. Fan response to "If You Ever Have Forever in Mind" was instantaneous and it began a fast rise up the country charts.

"It really surprised me that it's gotten embraced as well as it has. I appreciate the record company having the guts to take the chance."
—VINCE GILL

Excitement was building toward the August release of the complete album. His last offering, *High Lonesome*

Sound, had been quite different from his previous albums, so fans were even more geared up for *The Key*. They were also eager to check in with one of their favorite artists to see how he was doing. As everyone knew, 1997 had been a troubling year for Vince Gill in his personal life, and he had announced that he was taking some time off from touring and recording to deal with it.

In the spring of 1997, it was announced that Vince and his wife, Janis, who had gained fame in the 1980s as half of the singing duo Sweethearts of the Rodeo, were divorcing after seventeen years of marriage. At the time, he told reporters it was "a private and personal matter. And with all due respect I would like to keep it that way." He said he would never say a word about it. "I think it's disrespectful not only to myself but to everybody else involved."

A few months later, in July 1997, Vince's father, Stan Gill, died unexpectedly following surgery. For Vince, who has listed his parents as his heroes in press releases and fan club brochures, the loss was, as he later said in his quiet way, "a struggle." His fans really felt for his losses.

"I'm okay," he told a reporter. "I'm going to take nine months off, slow down, and regroup." He said he also wanted to spend more time with his teenage daughter, Jenny.

Country artists, like all musicians, spend a lot of time on the road, touring all over the United States and sometimes abroad to bring their music live and in person to the fans who graciously buy their records. Being off the road for many months gave Vince Gill the opportunity to work even more intensely on his songwriting, creating many new songs, thirteen of which would ultimately become *The Key*. How wonderful to be in Nashville, in the supportive warmth of the songwriting and music business community. What was even more rewarding was that Vince Gill was able to try out his new songs on the stage of the Grand Ole Opry.

Vince told reporters that this record was unlike anything he'd done. He said he missed doing the hard-core traditional country music. "That's what moves me," he said. "I miss the country music I remember. Losing my dad last year made me remember all the greats, like Buck Owens, Merle Haggard, and Patsy Cline—all those great country records with great country fills. This is where my heart is now and I let my heart lead me."

Those country fills are what make country music so much fun to listen to. They are those instrumental parts between the words, not necessarily a guitar or fiddle solo—although those are cool, too—but that pause where the guitar or pedal steel or fiddle or banjo "fills in."

Losing his dad made Vince look back over the forty years they were together and ask himself, "What did he teach? What did I learn?" He discovered that much of what his father had taught him was in those old songs.

Which brings us to the title cut, the most haunting song on the album. "The Key to Life" is a tribute to Stan Gill, Vince's beloved father. "That one is really sweet for me," Vince said, "because it really is the truth." The song talks about how Stan Gill taught his son to play three chords on the banjo when Vince was just a kid, and how that kid learned to play, practicing on many kinds of musical instruments until he grew up and went off to play music on the Opry stage. Evoking the titles of the songs his father loved—"John Henry," "Ol' Shep," "Faded Love," "I Fall to Pieces," and "On the Wings of a Dove"—Vince writes that even after he made it big, his father taught him one truth: All the riches and fame mean nothing if you don't remember who you really are.

"The neat thing about that song," Vince said, "is it says so many things that are the truth. I can't even describe how good it feels to see the truth written down on paper." It's a song written from the eyes of a boy through the pen of a man from the distance of a lifetime. This song shows the deep love Vince had for his father and raises a lump in the throat of anyone who's had a close relationship with his or her father. When Vince writes that he's honoring his father with the words he sings, there's no question he's honored his father's memory well.

When Vince was asked if *The Key* was autobiographical, it was a legitimate question. After all, the songs seemed to touch on a lot of things that could be related to his personal life. His answer was that part of it was, but that even the most personal of songs didn't have to be about him. "Everybody thinks you're showing all your cards," he said, "but you're not."

> "Vince has got to be the nicest person I have ever met in the music business. A fine musician and a great artist. He brings back the soul of country music like it used to be in the old days."
> —GEORGE JONES

You can talk about Vince Gill the artist almost forever—that's how good he is. But the other thing you'll always hear whenever you mention his name to anyone in Nashville is that he is the nicest guy around. For all of his talent and success, he truly does seem intent on following his father's advice to always remain himself and to never let it all go to his head. They say in the entertainment business that if you can learn to fake sincerity, you've got it made, but Vince Gill apparently couldn't fake sincerity if he tried. He's just naturally too sincere for that.

When asked about his philosophy of life, he once said, "Don't take anything too seriously." On another occasion he answered, "Be decent to people." He truly believes that integrity above all is the measure of the man.

"My integrity and what people think of me, along with how I've treated people, are important," he said. "Once you strip blue ribbons and all those awards and record sales, all you've got to be judged by is your character. That's all you can really want."

It's refreshing to see what really matters to the man who, throughout the 1990s, has earned more honors for his work than just about any other artist in country music. He just hasn't let his fame go to his head despite his great looks, compelling voice, musical virtuosity, and talent for songwriting. "I don't like this perception that you are just a little bit higher than this guy here," he said. "I hate egos. I'll fight forever not to show mine."

Now that's a change of pace—especially in the image-driven 1990s, when so many stars lost sight of who they were and what got them into the entertainment business in the first place. Though rock superstar Bruce Springsteen once warned his fans to "trust the art, not the artist," it's nice for fans to know that some artists really are the nice people they appear to be. Vince Gill seems to have always had his values in line.

One day he stopped in a record store while they just happened to be playing one of his albums. People couldn't stop staring at him. One woman asked him what he was doing there and he answered that he was there to buy some records. "I'll never get used to the recognition factor," he said. "I'm very approachable, very unassuming, and unlike some people, I try not to create a lot of hysteria."

Vince Gill lives a fairly normal life in Music City, a town where most citizens are thoroughly accustomed to seeing superstars in the supermarket. He drives a regular automobile, dresses like a regular guy, and goes to work like a regular guy—although his job is making music, either on his own albums or on those of other musicians. He plays basketball at the Y and plays golf as often as he can. In fact, if he weren't a professional musician, he'd very likely be a professional golfer. And his generosity in lending his name and his voice to a number of charitable causes has earned him the nickname "the king of benefits." He even calls his music publishing company Benefit Music.

At a press conference talking about *The Key*, Vince told the story of a woman who had approached him and handed him a piece of paper with a signature on it. It was Elvis Presley's autograph! Vince tried not to accept it, feeling she should keep that treasure for herself. But she insisted that she wanted Vince to have it. He said he keeps it "in a frame on top of his fridge, near the bacon." Elvis would love that his autograph is so close to his favorite food.

Vince is amazed when people want his autograph and thinks it's "pretty neat that people think that much about what you do." But if that's what the fans want, he's happy to do it. As Tony Brown has said, "He'll do anything—from getting up at six in the morning to do an interview to staying up till midnight signing autographs."

Being nice doesn't mean being anything less than devoted to the things that matter to him. "There are things that I'm intense about," he says. "I get on the guys if they're not playing as good as they can and should. I want things to be the best. I'm a perfectionist. I want everyone else to be equally committed." He's easygoing in his relations with the people he works with. It takes a lot of people to make an artist a star—record company employees, booking agents, publicists, music publishing executives, and business managers. "Everyone's got their area of expertise. Mine's writing songs, playing the guitar, and singing. I try to do that and let them do their jobs."

Recording an album is a real collaborative process between the producer and the singer and musicians. Generally, the producer's job is to help select the songs, hire the musicians, oversee all the song arrangements, the engineering, and the mixing of the master tape that will become the actual CD. Though it's obvious that Vince himself has a huge role in this process, his albums don't carry his name as a co-producer—a common practice with many artists. Tony Brown gets sole producer credit.

"I enjoy the record-making process as much as anything," Vince has said. "Music is not about hoarding it for yourself. The joy is letting people discover other people's talents."

As serious as he is about his music, Vince Gill has a great sense of humor, and he enjoys poking fun at everything, especially himself. Sometimes he sounds a little flip, but it's always in good taste.

As the beloved host of the annual nationally televised Country Music Association Awards, Vince Gill has brought his humor and great personality into the living rooms of millions of Americans. He has helped to make the show the second-highest-rated entertainment/variety show on the air—second only to the Oscars. It's a podium from which his humor really shines.

He's been hosting the CMA Awards for seven years. "I think they know that I'm gonna take it serious, but they also know I'm not gonna take it too serious," he says. "I guess that's why I get to keep doing it, because not only do I treat it with a great deal of respect, but I also have fun with it."

> "Vince has a genuine, humble, self-effacing personality. All those qualities are really hard to get in one person."
> —ED BENSON, executive director of the Country Music Association

"It's not about me trying to be the funniest guy in the biz," Vince says. "It's about me up there trying to showcase all of us with a lot of class and make everybody look good 'cause it's a win-win for everybody when the show comes off well."

"The bottom line is that the viewers love him," says Ed Benson. "We do audience research after the show every year, and he has an eighty-five percent audience rating approval. That's unheard-of in TV."

Walter Miller, the veteran producer of the CMA Awards show, says, "He just gets better and better. He's himself, no matter what he's doing, and I think that comes across."

Vince has joked that he could be called "the Hillbilly Crystal," referring to Billy Crystal's long stint as the beloved host of the Academy Awards. "I have a lot of fun with hosting," Vince said. "I have a few one-liners, but I have a great deal of reverence for the awards and for country music."

It really is all for the music with Vince Gill. As hard as he worked for his success, there are times when he doesn't believe it, because he never makes a big deal about himself.

"Look, I always knew I could make a living as a musician," he says. "I don't have to live in a mansion. I'm not a toy guy. I don't need a muscle car, a big boat, and a plane in the backyard. I've never invested in things. I invest in people."

> "I've never cared where I sat on the popularity poll or what my bank account says. I just want to play and sing."
>
> —VINCE GILL

He may not sing his own praises, but fellow musicians, critics, radio programmers, industry insiders, and especially the fans are proud to do so. For Vince Gill has accomplished far more than just becoming one of the best contemporary singers, songwriters, and musicians.

Vince Gill is a bridge between pop music, rock and roll, and country. He's an artist of his influences in the best possible way. From early country stars like Buck Owens, Chet Atkins, Patsy Cline, Lefty Frizzell, Bob Wills, and Merle Haggard, among many others, he developed his love for one of America's most cherished, homegrown art forms. He has absorbed the contemporary music of fifties icons like Frank Sinatra and Tony Bennett, sixties megastars like Bob Dylan and Eric Clapton, and seventies and eighties artists like Linda Ronstadt, The Eagles, and the various eclectic bands of Emmylou Harris. He hasn't copied anyone; instead, he has synergized all these influences and been able to draw on them to develop his own unique style and sound. His music makes the listener feel at home in a familiar place while experiencing something brand-new. What he's achieved is rare among any artist in any field of artistic pursuit.

> "The bottom line is that no matter what he does, you'll be seeing and hearing a lot from Vince for a long time."
>
> —TONY BROWN

Vince Gill has been playing music since he was five years old. Here is the story of how he got here from there.

CHAPTER TWO

Oklahoma Roots

"They had qualities of humor and courage and inventiveness and energy."

—JOHN STEINBECK,
writing about Oklahomans

The year was 1957. Elvis Presley was rocking radio all over America with his hot hit "All Shook Up." Buck Owens was generating a new sound in country music with his rough-and-tumble Bakersfield, California, honky tonk in a band featuring the amazing lead guitar sounds of Don Rich. Davey Crockett was on television, along with an array of other popular western shows. America was peaceful and prosperous and in the midst of a booming birth rate. Millions of children were being born and their impact on every aspect of our society in the decades to come could barely be imagined.

One of those new baby boomers was Vincent Grant Gill, born on April 12 in Norman, Oklahoma, twenty miles from Oklahoma City, right in the middle of the American heartland. He was the third child in the family of Stan and Jerene Gill.

Oklahoma's third-largest city, with a population today of 88,000, Norman was and still is a very family-oriented town. Its downtown is filled with beautiful, turn-of-the-century architecture, including the Sooner Theatre at 101 East Main. A treasure of Spanish Gothic architecture built in 1929 to take advantage of the new "talking pictures," it has been restored and today is the setting for community theater, dance performances, and concerts. A short distance away is the Norman Depot, until 1981 one of Oklahoma's premier railway stations and a symbol of the Santa Fe Railroad Company, whose tracks began running through Norman in 1887.

The University of Oklahoma, the town's major employer, was established seventeen years before Oklahoma achieved statehood. It offers the residents of Norman and greater Oklahoma City the Oklahoma Festival Ballet and the Modern Repertory Dance Theatre, both resident companies. The Cimarron Circuit Opera Company also has its home base in Norman.

"The guitar was his favorite toy."

—JERENE GILL

Most of the music Vince Gill heard as a very young child was right inside his own home. In Norman, and later in Oklahoma City, where the Gill family moved when Vince was four, music was an important part of life.

Stan Gill, Vince's father, played banjo and guitar and enjoyed performing in many of the small dance halls that were a part of community life in Oklahoma. Vince's mother, Jerene, a homemaker, played the piano and the harmonica. Vince's older brother, Bob, played the guitar as did his grandmother. His sister, Gena, says she is the only family member who wasn't bitten by the musical bug. The family spent a lot of time just sitting together and making music.

From the time he could walk, Vince loved to carry his grandmother's guitar around the house or hang it from a string around his neck.

"There was always music around the house," Vince said. If the Gills weren't making music of their own, they were playing their country music albums. On the radio, Vince heard all the great rock and roll of the 1950s and 1960s—and, of course, the country greats from the Grand Ole Opry.

The Grand Ole Opry has a wonderful history. In October 1925, the National Life and Accident Insurance Company inaugurated a radio station called WSM, the call letters named after the company's slogan, "We Shield Millions." George D. Hay, a former newspaperman and radio announcer who signed on as WSM's program director, had the idea for a live radio show featuring rural American music after visiting a similar show in the Ozark Mountains of Arkansas.

Hay called the show the "WSM Barn Dance," but the name was changed in 1928 when the host of a national opera show on the same station said the now-famous words, "For the past hour we have been listening to music taken largely from Grand Opera, but now we will present the Grand Ole Opry."

Vince later said that as a kid he had every record Chet Atkins ever made. "I marveled at how he played," Vince said. "He's the most effortless-looking musician I've ever seen." Atkins had begun playing the guitar at the age of nine, and by the time he left high school the seeds of his greatness had begun to sprout. He played on radio stations and made his Grand Ole Opry debut in 1946, the same year he began making records. Two years before Vince Gill was born, Chet Atkins had his first country hit as an instrumentalist with "Mr. Sandman." He was such an accomplished guitarist that Gibson Guitars was already commissioning him to create Chet Atkins guitars. As a consultant to and later head of the Nashville operation of RCA Victor, Atkins was, shall we say, instrumental, in the development of the great country talents of the 1960s and 1970s, bringing Charley Pride, Waylon Jennings, Don Gibson, and Floyd Cramer to the RCA roster. He also produced albums by artists like Eddy Arnold and Elvis Presley. "Country Gentleman" is one of his signature songs.

Local TV and radio shows like "Anthony Avenue," "Sooner Shindig," "Big Red Warehouse," and the "Chuck Wagon Gang" made it certain that lots of Oklahomans, young and old, got to hear plenty of great music all the time. It's no wonder Oklahoma has given country music—and other art forms—more than its share of great musical stars.

The Musical Stars of Oklahoma

Hoyt Axton • Garth Brooks • J. J. Cale
Henson Cargill • The Chainsaw Kittens
Charlie Christian • Color Me Badd
Joe Diffie • The Flaming Lips • David Gates
Vince Gill • Woody Guthrie • Hanson
Wade Hayes • Wanda Jackson • Harry James
Joose • Barney Kessel • Reba McEntire
The Nixons • Leon Russell • Kay Starr
B. J. Thomas • Jimmy Webb • Bryan White
Claude Williams • Mason Williams • Jeff Wood

You can't underestimate the importance of the music that was such a big part of Vince Gill's early life. In fact, almost all the musical artists in any genre, but most especially in country music, were exposed to music at a very early age and encouraged by their parents to appreciate it. Being taught that it's fun and even worthwhile to sit around playing music makes a child feel comfortable right from the start with dreaming about spending a lifetime in the field of music.

When he was only five years old, Vince Gill was strumming his first guitar. The first song he learned was "Ol' Shep." Not too long afterward, he learned "Long Tall Texan." By the time he was eight, he was good enough to play "Long Tall Texan" with his brother, Bob, at a local Oklahoma City radio station.

Like so many other kids, Vince took piano lessons. But the little formal training he had was less interesting to him than just learning to play by ear. "I got bored with theory," he said later. "Nothing stuck. I wanted to learn to play songs." He also took guitar lessons, and among his teachers was J. Julian Akins. Akins served his country in World War II. Afterward, he came home to Oklahoma City and became a staff guitarist for Oklahoma television and radio stations. He played with local bands and even played backup for such stars as Gene Autry.

Vince says he's had a guitar strapped around his neck for as long as he can remember. When he was ten, his parents bought him the first guitar that was his own. Once he started playing the guitar, he just couldn't put it down.

Music wasn't the only childhood activity that would last into adulthood for Vince Gill. Though the state of Oklahoma is completely landlocked, it has plenty of water. Flood control projects have created nearly two hundred reservoirs and more shoreline than on the Atlantic and Gulf Coasts combined. Lake Thunderbird near Norman, surrounded by the five-thousand-acre Lake Thunderbird State Park, was only one of the places families could go for summer fun. "We'd go carp fishing all the time, go swim for a while, eat french fries," Vince said. Sounds just fine. There was also a lot of time for sports including golf, baseball, and basketball.

Being the youngest of three children helped to make Vince Gill a mischievous child and the always smiling, funny guy he is today. He has spoken about the fact that everyone in his family had a great sense of humor and enjoyed just sitting around telling jokes.

> "That part of the country does have a sense of humor. There's a lot of charm to that, getting together with people and telling jokes."
>
> —VINCE GILL

On many occasions, Vince Gill has expressed his deep love for his home state. He has used the term *salt of the earth* to describe how the good, solid people of Oklahoma have retained their humor and common sense despite the many hard times they've endured.

The history of Oklahoma is in many ways the history of the United States. Located barely south of the exact center of the country, the state can be said to belong to the South due to its friendliness and hospitality, the Southwest as a result of its vast mesas and sun-baked towns, and the Midwest for its role as one of the top wheat producers in the country. But with its many saddle shops and men in cowboy boots and cowboy hats—not to mention more horses per capita than in any other state—Oklahoma is really a major part of the American West. For years it was known as the Indian Territory, where the members of the thirty-seven Native American nations came together after the southeastern tribes were forced to relocate there. Today, Oklahoma is home to more Native Americans than any other state.

On April 22, 1889, a crowd of ten thousand people gathered at the edge of the Unassigned Lands in Central Oklahoma. Hopeful homesteaders lined up on horseback and bicycles, in wagons and on foot, coming from all over the United States and even from as far away as Italy, Czechoslovakia, and England. The Great Land Run began with cannon fire, but some people snuck in a little sooner than that, which resulted in Oklahoma's nickname as the Sooner State.

Both of his parents were raised on farms, though Vince has remarked that he doesn't share the legacy of growing up poor and struggling of many country singers. He grew up in a typical middle-class family.

"Growing up in Oklahoma City," he has said, "was just normal. Both my parents had a good grasp on common sense and a strong sense of right and wrong." Vince was raised with plenty of discipline and also the freedom to make his own decisions.

He attended grade school at Grover Cleveland and used to bring his guitar to school for show-and-tell. He liked to play it and sing "House of the Rising Sun," among many other songs popular at the time. His classmates knew he was serious about playing guitar.

When he was nine years old, Vince played golf for the first time. His father was a weekend golfer and Vince, in the third grade, was becoming a bit of a golf nut himself.

"As juniors, we could play for twenty-five cents or thirty-five cents," he said. "Mom said golf was the best baby-sitter in the world."

Vince also loved basketball, baseball, and football from an early age. "I practiced music and sports all the time," he said. Some of his classmates say he was pretty competitive when it came to sports.

The basement of the Gill home in Oklahoma City became Vince's first recording studio when he was in junior high school. He and his father made a recording of John Denver's hit "Take Me Home, Country Roads." Vince says, "It's the first tape I have of me singing." Up until then, Vince had only played guitar or the other instruments he was becoming proficient at—the banjo, Dobro, and mandolin. Stan Gill once said that Vince didn't start singing until he was about thirteen and figured out how much the girls liked it. Vince confirmed it. "By junior high, gosh, you did find out that girls liked boys who sang and played guitar."

What kind of records was he buying then at the stores? "I can't remember if the first record I actually bought with my own money was by the Beatles or 'They're Coming to Take Me Away,' " Vince said.

But even then he took a different approach than most kids his age. "I paid more attention to the musicians when I was young. It was fun for me," he said. "I bought records because of who was playing on them."

A broken banjo string became a turning point in the early musical career of Vince Gill.

Vince was playing his dad's banjo one day when a string popped. Wanting to get it fixed, Vince called a friend of his father's, Charlie Clark, who said to bring the banjo on over. It turns out that Charlie's teenage son,

Bobby, was a mandolin player who played a lot of blue-grass music.

Vince had grown up hearing bluegrass, mostly on the Grand Ole Opry radio broadcasts the Gill family listened to on Saturday nights. It was great music, but probably not the kind that one would expect to earn a living with in the age of dreamy pop and hard rock.

"I didn't care if someone thought I was a geek because I wouldn't drink a beer or because I played bluegrass music."

—VINCE GILL

In the mid-1970s, bluegrass music was not exactly in the forefront of American popular culture, but then again, it never has been. The beautiful sounds of high tenor voices singing crystal-clear harmonies to the music of mandolins, guitars, fiddles, bass fiddles, and, of course, banjos, came from the hills of Appalachia in the south-eastern United States. It was in the hollers, the deep hollow spaces between mountains that were technically valleys but were really too small to be called valleys, that bluegrass was born. The unique sound was sometimes called mountain music because, back then, even if the hill people had radios, they couldn't really get much reception. So they created their own music, based on the English, Irish, and Scottish tunes and melodies they re-membered from their homelands and on the distinctive sounds of the songs they sang in church. Many bluegrass songs have deep religious roots. Certainly the two-, three-, and four-part harmonies that are so distinctive to blue-grass and its unique high-pitched tenor singing could be heard in churches all across Appalachia.

Bill Monroe may not have invented bluegrass music, but he certainly gave it its name and became its best-known player and spokesman. Monroe was born and raised in Rosine, Kentucky, a town where visitors today are greeted by a sign that says, "Hi There. Welcome to Rosine—Home of Bluegrass Music." Monroe's parents both died when he was relatively young, leading, some say, to the sadness that underlies so many of his songs. He was raised, and taught to play music, by his great uncle Pendleton Vandiver, whom he immortalized in one of his best-known songs, "Uncle Pen."

In October 1938, Monroe made a recording of what would ultimately become his trademark song, "Mule Skinner Blues." Though his first band was called the Kentuckians, Bill Monroe wasn't happy with that name. Perhaps unaware he was coining a word that would become synonymous with the purest of musical sounds, he changed the name of his band to Bill Monroe and the Blue Grass Boys. They traveled throughout the South in their car, the "Blue Grass Special," spreading the musical sounds of the Appalachian Mountains. They also spent considerable time playing baseball to stretch their legs after so many hours in the car.

"That's what America's all about for me."
          —BOB DYLAN, on the music of Bill Monroe

Monroe's lyrics were simply written, touching tales of the pleasures of living on a farm, the hardships of tough economic times, and the heartbreaks of loss and betrayal. His music was far more complex than the lyrics—deliberately structured to make room for the instruments that were played with astonishing speed and precision.

Monroe was a master at the mandolin. Many fiddlers, pickers, and strummers learned their craft playing with Monroe and his band, including Oklahoman Byron Berline, winner of the National Fiddle Championship. Two other gifted musicians, singer Lester Flatt and banjo player Earl Scruggs, played with the Blue Grass Boys until 1948. They left to form their own band, the Foggy Mountain Boys, which became another of the all-time great bluegrass groups, touring the countryside in their bus emblazoned with the logo of their sponsor, the Martha White Flour Company.

Along with Bill Monroe and the Blue Grass Boys and Flatt and Scruggs, the Stanley Brothers—Carter and Ralph—were gaining fame as the house band for many local radio stations with *their* group, the Clinch Mountain Boys, named for the rugged Clinch Mountain county of Dickinson in Virginia. For twenty years they toured extensively and recorded numerous albums until Carter died in 1966 at the early age of forty-one. Fortunately, Ralph decided to continue with the Clinch Mountain Boys during a time when bluegrass festivals were becoming increasingly popular. By the mid-1970s, there were dozens of albums featuring their great brand of bluegrass, which put more emphasis on the guitar than on the traditional mandolin.

Bluegrass remained just as isolated as the Appalachian hollers where it was created. This helped retain the purity and beauty of the music, which, in turn, kept the fans and musicians excited about it. Good thing, because big record companies and most radio stations have never really supported bluegrass music. Only the fans and musicians have kept it alive. Bluegrass is not the same as country music mainly because it has always stayed close to its beginnings. In many ways, it is really indigenous American folk music. In the 1940s and 1950s, bluegrass deeply influenced the newer folk music of people like Pete Seeger, Woody Guthrie, and the Weavers, among others, who took bluegrass elements and added their own political messages to the music. In turn, these artists influenced the folk music of people like Bob Dylan and Joan Baez, who influenced almost all the music that came after them.

The broken string on Stan Gill's banjo was replaced and Vince gained a new friend and fellow musician in Bobby Clark.

"I'd never played any bluegrass," Vince said, "and I started learning about it." He loved the structure of the harmonies and, as a guitar player, instantly took to the freedom bluegrass music gave each musician to play solos any way he wanted to. And even though he didn't really consider himself a singer at the time, the high tenor harmonies of bluegrass and Vince Gill's voice seemed a match made in heaven.

When Vince was attending Northwest Classen High School in Oklahoma City, he worked on a golf course and at a pizza place. The strong work ethic instilled in him as a child would serve him well in later years. He also played in a rock band. "I was just trying to be one of the boys in Led Zeppelin," he said, referring to one of the loudest and most acclaimed rock bands of all time. The local rock band had called Vince and asked him to play banjo. Plenty of people thought it was pretty cool to see a banjo player in a rock band. Vince was also able to play electric guitar with that band. "I thought I was Jimi Hendrix, too," he said, not realizing at the time that one day people would regard him as the late, great rock guitarist's equal in making the instrument sing.

One time one of Vince's bands was going to play at a school assembly. He called a friend and asked him to play a Doobie Brothers song on the phone. The friend played it a few times and a few days later Vince was able to play it flawlessly for the assembly.

"I would think that bluegrass music in 1974 or 1975, when you were a sophomore in high school, could be considered very uncool," Vince said. But Vince cared about the music. He didn't care about being cool. Everyone liked him anyway. The hippies liked him because he played electric guitar in a dance band. The jocks liked him because he was a decent athlete. He still played golf all the time, but even though he was good at kicking field goals, he didn't want to be on the football team. "I was the manager and flirted with the cheerleaders. That was a lot more fun than having your brains knocked out all the time."

When Vince was in his teens, he heard a Linda Ronstadt album. He was impressed with Ronstadt and also with the voice of the woman singing harmony with Linda on the song "I Can't Help It (If I'm Still in Love with You)." Vince checked the album cover and saw that the harmony singer was named Emmylou Harris. For some reason, he was convinced the singer was Dolly Parton using a fake name. But soon after that he found a copy of Emmylou Harris's *Pieces of the Sky* album. Vince was immediately drawn to her voice and her music.

The kid had great taste in music. Emmylou Harris grew up in North Carolina and Virginia, the daughter of a career U.S. marine. She played saxophone in high school but when she discovered folk music, she knew she had found her musical passion. That music drew her to the cross-roads of Bleecker and MacDougal Streets in New York City's Greenwich Village in the mid-sixties. There she played in the many folk clubs and coffeehouses while working as a waitress. These were the clubs where, only a few years before, folk artists like Bob Dylan, Joan Baez, Eric Andersen, Tim Hardin, and others were changing music, culture, and politics all at the same time. By the early 1970s, Emmylou was living in Washington, D.C., and playing at such landmark D.C.-area clubs as the Cellar Door, Clydes, and the Red Fox. It was here that she met Chris Hillman and Gram Parsons of the Flying Burrito Brothers. Parsons had helped form the Flying Burrito Brothers in 1968, and when Emmylou met him, he had just left the group.

Like Harris, Parsons had also played folk music and protest songs in Greenwich Village, beginning when he was sixteen years old. He'd belonged to the folk group Shiloh and was also a member of the Byrds, persuading that group to move from their folk-rock roots to a more country sound. (The Byrds' album *Sweetheart of the Rodeo* is considered by many to be the first real country rock album.) Parsons urged Emmylou to take another look at the music of her native South and she sang harmony on his solo debut album, *Gram Parsons*, in 1972, perhaps not aware initially of the historic role she was playing in Parsons's trailblazing fusion of country and rock. Many top session players, including bluegrass fiddler Byron Berline, contributed to that album. Harris recorded a second album with Parsons, *Grievous Angel*, whose players also included Berline as well as the remarkable young singer Linda Ronstadt and Herb Pedersen, who would later form the Desert Rose Band.

Gram Parsons died suddenly in September 1973. The music world lost one of its most daring and original members and Emmylou Harris lost her great mentor. She put her own band together and, in 1975, released the album that had grabbed Vince Gill's attention, *Pieces of the Sky*.

Vince was having fun playing two kinds of music—hard rock and bluegrass—and he was great at both. Since some of the bluegrass bands wouldn't play at clubs that served liquor, Vince played the rowdier places with his rock band. The band he was in with Bobby Clark was considered one of the more serious bluegrass bands in Oklahoma City, so he was able to really polish his acoustic guitar skills as well as his work on the mandolin and Dobro. It didn't take long for word to get around that this high school boy was one heck of a musician.

Word got to Mountain Smoke, Oklahoma's premiere bluegrass band, and they asked Vince to join as a vocalist and lead guitarist. The other guys were all ten or twelve years older than Vince.

"I'd have to say it was the most fun I ever had playing music," he said. "What an amazing set of personalities." Mountain Smoke was made up of a college student, a sprinkler installer, a music professor, two bankers, and Northwest Classen High School student Vince Gill. "I was seventeen and hanging out with these men—all grown up with families and crazy as a bunch of loons. I had a lot of firsts in the year I was with 'em."

One of those firsts was hearing himself on the radio singing a song he and Mountain Smoke had recorded. It was a cut from a Mountain Smoke album that Vince's mother still has a copy of—after all, her son's picture is on the cover. Vince was so excited he called all his friends on his CB radio and told them to turn on their radios to listen.

Mountain Smoke played a lot of their own shows, but they also opened for national acts coming through Oklahoma City. One night some concert promoters called to ask Mountain Smoke to fill in for an opening act that had canceled at the last minute. Vince and the guys hopped in the car and drove down. "I remember seeing the marquee that said KISS and thought, hmmm, they must be playing here tomorrow night," he said.

In their wild costumes and Japanese kabuki-style makeup, the band called KISS was known for wild live shows complete with amazing pyrotechnics and outrageous stage antics. Their fans came out expecting nothing less than a full-scale blowout of dazzling sights and eardrum-piercing sounds.

Mountain Smoke got on stage and started playing pure bluegrass. The KISS fans didn't like that at all. In fact, before long the crowd was booing. Vince tried his best to be polite, saying "Thank ye kindly" after every song, but his band was drowned out by the audience's unrestrained expression of displeasure.

"It was kind of exciting getting booed by that many people."

—VINCE GILL

Vince said he figured if he was a hard-rock-and-roll fan and some little old bluegrass band came out and started playing for him, he wouldn't like it, either. Still, imagine the sound of five thousand people booing all at once and it's no wonder some of the guys in Mountain Smoke started getting nervous. They managed to play four or five songs before the crowd started throwing things.

Sometimes a guy's got to do what a guy's got to do, and

Vince did. As the reviewer for the *Tulsa World* so tactfully put it, "Vince Gill showed what part of his anatomy the crowd could kiss." Apparently the police at the show liked what Vince did. They gave him a standing ovation. Later, Vince told an interviewer what he'd done was to give "the international symbol for disrespect."

Years later, some of Oklahoma City's musicians were still talking about Vince showing the fans of rock's wildest band that they shouldn't mess around with him.

Mountain Smoke survived that night and continued playing in the area. One night they opened for the pop group Pure Prairie League.

Formed in 1970 in Cincinnati, Ohio, Pure Prairie League took its name from a women's temperance group in the Errol Flynn movie *Dodge City*. The band was distinctive in a number of ways. The original members—guitarist George Powell, steel guitar player John David Call, sidemen Jim "Koffe" Caughlin and Jim Lanham, and lead singer/songwriter/guitarist Craig Fuller—combined the best of pop, country rock, and bluegrass to create a sound that fit perfectly into the musical tastes of the late sixties and early seventies. The band was mostly acoustic with steel guitar playing and pure country sounds enhancing their pop and rock songs. They were influenced by such groups as the Byrds and Creedence Clearwater Revival. A lot of different kinds of bands were making Cincinnati a serious music scene at the time, and it wasn't long before Pure Prairie League was one of the most popular acts at Billy's, one of the hottest clubs in town. That's where they met drummer Billy Hinds, who joined the band in 1972, as did Mike Reilly and keyboardist Michael Connor. RCA signed them and their first two albums, *Pure Prairie League* and *Bustin' Out*, apart from containing great music, introduced the band's symbol, a little cowboy named Luke, taken from a Norman Rockwell *Saturday Evening Post* painting.

When Pure Prairie League brought their unique blend of rock and country music to Oklahoma City, the members of Mountain Smoke not only opened for them, they went out and played with them on stage. "We had a real good time with them that night," Vince said. "We smoked 'em. The paper said something about how the local guys had outshone the headliners."

It was the summer of 1975 and Vince Gill had just graduated from high school. His interests were well-developed—he loved music and he loved golf and he was pretty darn good at both of them. Now came a kind of turning point, one of those moments that just happen and that can determine the rest of your life—or at least the next twenty years.

"I wish I could say that Oklahoma State was beating down my door to come play on a golf scholarship," Vince said, "but they weren't."

But somebody else did beat on his door. It was Sam Bush, the fiddle player from the progressive bluegrass group Bluegrass Alliance. Word of Vince's bluegrass skills had traveled to Louisville, Kentucky. Now Bush was asking him to join one of the most prominent bluegrass bands of the mid-1970s.

He was only eighteen. His parents were a little worried about their son taking off to go play in a band so far from home. Still, they knew enough about music to know how talented their son was and that this chance to join Bluegrass Alliance was a good opportunity.

Vince was secure enough in his talent to take the chance

and secure enough in his family to know that if it didn't work out, he could always come home.

So in the summer of 1975, Vince Gill packed all his stuff into a van and headed east to Louisville, the very heart of bluegrass country. He'd take his guitar skills and his growing excellence on the mandolin and banjo and give it a shot. Maybe he could make it as a professional musician.

CHAPTER THREE

Kentucky Bluegrass
to California Pop

"Some of the people I got to play with in bluegrass music back then were huge and the
whole time was great for me."

—VINCE GILL

Sam Bush could play the mandolin and fiddle like a
wild man. He'd play hard, he'd play long, and he'd take
those instruments to places no one else had tried to take
them before. Fully immersed in bluegrass, he was always
pushing it in new directions and constantly experimenting
with various other forms of music. This was natural for a
guy who had bought his first mandolin at the age of eleven
before taking up the fiddle and winning fifth place on his
first try at the National Old Time Fiddle Contest in Idaho.

He was also the guy who wanted to take the important
bluegrass group that had been formed in 1967, the Bluegrass Alliance, to even more progressive heights. He'd already been around for the group's biggest hit, "One Tin
Soldier," a song that was renamed "The Legend of Billy
Jack" and used as background music for the hit cult movie

Billy Jack in 1971. Bush also helped form New Grass Revival.

Bush saw in Vince Gill a talent far beyond his years. Vince knew more about bluegrass than most young musicians in the mid-1970s and was ready to soak up all he could learn about the music he loved. "Bluegrass influenced the way I approach music," he said. "I love those days. It was good training ground." Vince's proficiency on guitar, fiddle, banjo, Dobro, and mandolin just about made him a one-man bluegrass band.

Vince wasn't the only baby boomer discovering bluegrass. In 1975, just as Vince Gill was getting started in Kentucky, a bluegrass mandolin whiz named David Grisman released an album called *Old and in the Way*, which had been recorded at the Boarding House in San Francisco. The album featured a host of great musicians including Vassar Clements on fiddle, John Khan on bass, and the one and only Jerry Garcia of the Grateful Dead on banjo. Grisman had started out with the Even Dozen Jug Band in New York and then moved to San Francisco, playing with such singular musicians as Maria Muldaur and John Sebastian. This album made a jazz, rock, and pop public aware of the beauty of mandolin, and for at least part of that audience it became a trailmarker to bluegrass. In the late 1970s, Grisman was bringing live bluegrass to jazz clubs and to rock audiences as an opening act for the major rock stars of the time like Neil Young and the Eagles.

If Vince Gill had chosen to go to the finest university with the most distinguished research professors to study his chosen profession, he could not have done better than he did by going to Kentucky in 1975. As a member of the Bluegrass Alliance with Sam Bush and another noted bluegrasser, Dan Crary, he was learning from the best. Bluegrass festivals were everywhere, featuring bands like the Seldom Scene and the Dillards and musicians like the great bluegrass traditionalist Del McCoury. Vince played on shows with Bill Monroe and the Blue Grass Boys, Ralph Stanley and the Clinch Mountain Boys, and with the Earl Scruggs Revue, formed by Scruggs with his sons Gary, Randy, and Steve after Flatt and Scruggs ended their long run as bluegrass champions. Vince began a friendship with Randy Scruggs that lasts to this day. He met Herb Pedersen, a longtime bluegrass musician who was a big fan of Flatt and Scruggs and the Stanley Brothers. Well-respected bluegrass and country player Mac Wiseman was also part of the bluegrass scene.

Vince did some work with the Bluegrass Revue, whose members included his old friend, world champion mandolin player Bobby Clark, and other bluegrass masters like banjo player Bill Perry, stand-up bass player Mike Perry, and guitarist David Bonham, among others.

In Kentucky, Vince also met two young musicians who, like himself, had gravitated to music as soon as they could pick up an instrument.

Keith Whitley was born in 1955 in the Big Sandy Valley of eastern Kentucky and grew up listening to the traditional country music of such greats as Hank Williams and George Jones. He was playing excellent lead guitar and singing at a very young age. A few counties away, another young boy was dazzling his neighbors with his own amazing skills on the mandolin. Ricky Skaggs was so good that before he was seven years old, he'd been on stage with Bill Monroe and the Blue Grass Boys showing the Father of Bluegrass that he could really play. By the time he was eight, Ricky was a master guitar player and then, in his teens, mastered the fiddle and electric guitar.

Both Keith Whitley and Ricky Skaggs were making the circuit of the many talent shows in Kentucky, so it was only a matter of time before they would meet. They became friends and began performing together, creating a group called the East Kentucky Mountain Boys, with a sound similar to that of Ralph Stanley and the Clinch Mountain Boys. Fate brought them to the attention of Ralph Stanley, and soon Keith and Ricky were performing regularly with the Clinch Mountain Boys. Each also spent time playing with several of the many bluegrass bands in the area, including Country Gentlemen and J. D. Crowe and the New South.

In 1975, after taking some time off from music to work in a boiler room for the Virginia Electric Power Company in Washington, D.C., Ricky Skaggs formed his own bluegrass group called Boone Creek. Breaking with the purists, he added drums, electric guitar, and piano to the traditional bluegrass instruments. One of the members of Boone Creek, for a while, was Vince Gill.

Vince played bass and steel guitar with Boone Creek in 1975 and 1976, honing his skills on a few more instruments. (Is there anything this guy can't play?) With Boone Creek, Vince continued to play in various clubs, hotels, and bluegrass haunts all through the South. But soon, he and Skaggs bumped heads a bit, not a big surprise when you put two intensely talented musicians in the same band. Vince reportedly wanted to sing all the lead parts and Ricky objected. "I started complaining incessantly," Vince said, "and eventually drove myself out of the band."

Then Vince got a phone call from another master musician. Another native Oklahoman, Byron Berline, offered

Vince a great opportunity—and soon he packed up his van and hit the road again. This time his destination was sunny Southern California.

Byron Berline was born in 1944 and grew up in Grant County, Oklahoma. His father was a highly accomplished fiddle player, his mother played piano, and his brother played guitar. When he was five he learned to play dance tunes on a fiddle that came from the Montgomery Ward catalog, and throughout his childhood he and his family played at fiddling contests, church suppers, PTA meetings—anywhere folks gathered and wanted to hear a little pickin'.

While attending the University of Oklahoma in 1963, Berline met the Dillards, the renowned bluegrass group who, among other accomplishments, became the fictitious bluegrass-playing "Darlin Family" on "The Andy Griffith Show." That show introduced many Americans to bluegrass music for the first time. Berline started playing with the Dillards and became the star attraction on their album *Pickin' and Fiddlin'*. After winning three consecutive National Fiddle Championships in the 1960s, he played the 1965 Newport Folk Festival, where he met Bob Dylan and Bill Monroe. Later, Berline played with Bill Monroe and the Blue Grass Boys for about a year.

After serving time in the army, Berline moved to Los Angeles in 1969 to continue working with the Dillards and with Gene Clark, who was a founding member of the Byrds. Word of his astonishing fiddling skills spread, and over the next several years his distinctive sound could be heard on albums by the Flying Burrito Brothers, the Byrds, Barry McGuire, Stephen Stills, Gram Parsons, the Nitty Gritty Dirt Band, and many others. Meanwhile, he was touring with the Flying Burrito Brothers. Berline and some other members of the Flying Burrito Brothers created a bluegrass band called Country Gazette that played a roaring bluegrass set in the middle of each Flying Burrito Brothers concert. Country Gazette toured in Europe, making a significant contribution to the popularity of bluegrass and country rock that continues today in many European countries.

By 1975, Byron Berline had grown tired of touring, so he decided to put together his own band. Country Gazette turned into Sundance and it featured some top musicians, including Dan Crary on guitar; Jack Skinner on bass and banjo; John Hickman on banjo, guitar, and mandolin; Allen Wald on guitar; and Skip Conover on Dobro and guitar. In 1976, Jack Skinner was fixing to leave the group. That's when Byron Berline called his fellow Oklahoman Vince Gill to come and join the band as its guitar player. Like so many in the 1930s, this young Oklahoman hoped that California held the key to his future. He was nineteen years old.

Vince played with Byron Berline and Sundance for about two years, getting to know the Los Angeles music scene and letting all the great session players and recording artists get to know his awesome talent. At the time, Byron Berline was contributing his amazing fiddle playing to such major albums as *Northern Lights, Southern Cross* by the Band, the legendary group that mixed elements of country with rock and roll, and he'd appeared on Emmylou Harris's *Pieces of the Sky*. One hallmark of true musicians is their constant desire to play great music—it doesn't matter whether its on their own albums or the albums of others, these guys just want to play and be part of excellent shows or sessions. Vince was able to see in Berline the kind of musician he might want to be in the future. Berline was busy in 1976 and 1977, working on albums like Jonathan Edwards's *Rockin' Chair*, Kris Kristofferson's *Surreal Thing*, Olivia Newton-John's *Making a Good Thing Better*, *Elite Hotel* by Emmylou Harris, and albums by James Taylor, Arlo Guthrie, and a very talented new singer/songwriter, Rodney Crowell.

Vince Gill wasn't the first baby boomer to head west to the promised land of California. By the mid-1970s, with the Vietnam War over and millions of boomers hitting their early twenties, there was a huge westward migration. America's new generation felt strong after having protested the war, proud that its insistence on equality and justice had advanced the women's rights and civil rights movements, and eager to experience the freedom of being over twenty-one. California was the land of all sorts of new explorations of that freedom. Nowhere was this freedom more evident than in the music. The Eagles were singing about love and liberation. Loggins and Messina were showing us how to party. The Grateful Dead were celebrating the hippie life and finding millions who wanted to celebrate with them.

When Byron Berline arrived in 1969 to play with the Dillards, that group had already been making substantial inroads in the Los Angeles folk scene. The hip rockers and crooners of L.A. were getting turned on to bluegrass, America's homegrown folk music. When the Flying Burrito Brothers released *The Gilded Palace of Sin*, hip rock and country folk came together in one new sound. Some people called this music "long-haired country."

Rock and roll was still strong (always was, always will be!) and its rebellious spirit was fueling even more political activism. Many cultural changes that began in California were also spreading all over the United States.

In the late 1970s, America had a southerner in the White House, Jimmy Carter. For the first time, a president was enjoying the support of rock and roll musicians. The Allman Brothers, Linda Ronstadt, the Eagles, and others held rallies and fund-raisers for the new president. America was also in the midst of an oil crisis. Auto plants in Detroit were laying off workers and the promise of jobs in Atlanta and Texas was drawing these laid-off northern factory workers to the South and Southwest. A lot of these people were real rock fans, and their love of music created a new audience for country rock.

Up to this point, country music had been completely traditional, and with a few exceptions, the audience was white and conservative. But you couldn't discount the influence of Jerry Lee Lewis, Carl Perkins, and, of course, Elvis Presley, who not only were on the rock charts but were finding their way to the country charts as well. The new country artists coming up couldn't help but be influenced by these pillars of rock and roll as well as by Hank Williams and Jimmy Rodgers. Another phenomenon around this time was the appearance of the crowd known in Nashville as the outlaws: Waylon Jennings, Willie Nelson, and Merle Haggard. Even though Willie wrote "Crazy" for Patsy Cline, it took the baby boomers who listened to the Rolling Stones to help Willie gain wider acclaim and success as a performer and a recording artist. These outlaws played their music straight from the heart, and at the time, when country was filled with strings and lush arrangements, it was difficult for them to find a place on radio. Their lifestyles were more rock and roll than country and they probably played the most authentic American music of their time. In 1976, Waylon Jennings and Willie Nelson received the Single of the Year award from the Country Music Association for "Good Hearted Woman." Song of the Year was awarded to songwriter Larry Weiss for "Rhinestone Cowboy," performed by Glen Campbell. Country was changing as much as everything else was.

In the new American south and out in California, cultures that were seemingly at odds were blending. Groups like Buffalo Springfield, Poco, the Byrds, and the Nitty Gritty Dirt Band were finding audiences from all of these cultures. By 1976, the Eagles had taken this new country rock music to new heights. In their music, fans in all parts of the country were hearing the influence of Motown, rhythm and blues, Delta blues, southern soul and gospel, cajun, country, and bluegrass.

What a fertile and exciting time for Vince Gill to be in California. His thick, brown hair was curling down around his shoulders. He was hanging out and playing with some of the best musicians around, the purveyors of a thinking man's country. He took to the California music scene like he'd been born to it. And he got the chance to witness the huge changes taking place in the business of music.

Suddenly music artists were commanding audiences that could only be accommodated in large arenas and stadiums, where hockey and football games were played the day before a big concert. These were the new places to share the excitement of live, loud music with twenty thousand of your closest friends. But they were not conducive and the technology wasn't advanced enough to showcase close harmonies and acoustic instruments. For groups playing that kind of music, the clubs were still the place to be. Places like the Bottom Line and Bitter End in New York, the Cellar Door in Washington, D.C., the Great American Music Hall in San Francisco, and the Troubador in Los Angeles were where music fans could always find a bluegrass or country act, sometimes wedged in between more modern rock acts such as the young Bruce Springsteen and other emerging music, like the punk scene from England. It was also in these clubs that fans could still hear Byron Berline, Doc Watson, the Dillards, the Souther-Hillman-Furay band, the great a cappella group the Persuasions, and even on occasion Emmylou Harris, who had outgrown the clubs and could now be found in the two-thousand-seat concert halls. Although these acts were every bit as talented and unique as those filling the stadiums, they never dominated radio to the degree necessary to advance to that level. Around this time, Rodney Crowell, a Houston, Texas, singer/songwriter was becoming a staple on the club circuit.

> "A lot of times I'd end up playing on the pier out in California, opening up the guitar case with my buddies and playing for tips. It's as much fun as playing in front of fifteen thousand people."
>
> —VINCE GILL

One evening, Vince Gill and Byron Berline and the Sundance band were playing a show at the Troubador, the hot club in L.A. at the time. Legend has it that it was at the Troubador that songwriters Glenn Frey, Jackson Browne, and J. D. Souther met. It's where Linda Ronstadt heard a group called the Longbranch Pennywhistle—which would evolve into the Eagles—and asked them to be her backup band. The Troubador was a musicians' and music industry hangout on the corner of Santa Monica Boulevard and Doheny. Alliances would be forged at the bar and deals would be closed next door at the famous Dan Tana's restaurant.

There were some special guests in the audience the night Sundance was playing the Troubador. Dolly Parton was at the height of her career and had been the CMA Female Vocalist of the Year for 1975 and 1976. Emmylou Harris and Rodney Crowell were also there. One of the songs Sundance sang was "Til' I Gain Control," written by Rodney Crowell.

"Rodney came up to me afterward and said, 'Oh, by the way, I'm Rodney Crowell and I wrote that song,' " Vince remembered. "He paid me some really fine compliments and that's where our friendship started."

In September 1978, Vince accompanied a friend to a studio in L.A. where Pure Prairie League was rehearsing.

Despite everything they'd had going for them in the early 1970s, Pure Prairie League's albums weren't successful enough for a big label and they were dropped. Craig Fuller had become a conscientious objector, refusing, like many others, to go to war in Vietnam. The legal consequences caused him to leave the group. Larry Goshorn joined the band as a lead singer and guitarist and Pure Prairie League did their best to keep going without a record deal by playing colleges all over the country. And then one of those weird and wonderful things happened that restore our faith in the power of good music to overcome the odds.

A song named "Amie," written by Craig Fuller and recorded on the *Bustin' Out* album, was gaining a following among college students, who began requesting it from radio stations. Radio stations forced RCA to release it as a single and, in 1975, three years after the album's release, "Amie" became a Top 30 hit. That prompted RCA to re-sign Pure Prairie League. Their comeback album, *Two Lane Highway*, featured performances by such giants as Chet Atkins, Emmylou Harris, Don Felder of the Eagles, and master fiddler Johnny Gimble. The title track reached the Top 100. The group was now touring constantly. They had recorded two more albums—*Dance* and *If the Shoe Fits*—and had a radio hit with their version of Buddy Holly's classic "That'll Be the Day." In 1977, they released a widely acclaimed live set called *Live Takin' the Stage*. After that, there were some personnel changes in the band and Pure Prairie League, now based in Los Angeles, was looking to regroup.

Vince hadn't seen the group in five or six years, not since he'd been with Mountain Smoke in high school and the Oklahoma City band had been Pure Prairie League's opening act. "I asked them if they remembered me," he said. "They said, 'Yeah, you're the kid from Oklahoma who played all the instruments.'"

Although Vince wasn't looking for a gig and had in fact just gone along with a friend who was auditioning, Pure Prairie League offered him the job on the spot. He wasn't interested at first but decided to try it for a couple of weeks to see if it was any fun. It must have been, because soon Vince Gill was Pure Prairie League's new guitarist, fiddler, and banjo player as well as lead vocalist.

Though Vince was "the countriest singer they could get," as he put it, Pure Prairie League was concentrating more on pop than they had before. Still, the opportunity he was being offered was incredible for someone so young. For the next three or four years, Vince would tour in style. He would become part of the progressive music scene and come to love the freedom the West Coast offered. He would also be part of studio recording sessions where, for the first time, he didn't have to count every penny the way the bluegrass groups had to.

After he'd been working with Pure Prairie League for a while, Vince pulled out the review from the Oklahoma City show when Mountain Smoke had opened for them. He showed them how the reviewer had said Mountain Smoke outplayed Pure Prairie League. It was all in good fun, and the brash young Vince got a kick out of teasing his new band.

> "During that time I gained knowledge that I used over the next fifteen years in the music business. Pure Prairie League was my college."
> —VINCE GILL

He also got a chance he hadn't even dreamed of. After RCA released *Can't Hold Back* in 1979, Pure Prairie League moved to Casablanca Records for their next album.

"Pure Prairie League was going into the studio and asked me if I had written any songs," Vince said. He had written seven. "I said, 'Yeah,' and we recorded five of 'em." The album was called *Firin' Up*, released in 1980. It is a testament to Vince that the more experienced musicians in the group recognized his talent, seeing the seeds of the great artist to come.

The first single, "Let Me Love You Tonight," featured Vince Gill on lead vocals. It reached number eight on the pop charts and number one on adult contemporary—the highest charting song of Pure Prairie League's career. The second single was "I'm Almost Ready." Written by Vince, it made it as far as number thirty-four. This song in particular foreshadows the unique style and phrasing that would mature into today's familiar and well-loved Vince

Gill sound. There is a hint of the higher tenor to come in Vince's voice, though he sings this tune in a range that is somewhat lower than the sound we hear today. Two other songs written by Vince, "I'll Be Damned" and "Janny Lou," also appeared on *Firin' Up*.

Pure Prairie League started touring even more. They were on TV, playing on "American Bandstand" and "Solid Gold." Right in front, there was Vince Gill—singing his heart out, playing like the dickens, looking like lots of other young guys of the time—like a real hippie. "Here I was this bluegrass picker," Vince said. "I guess some people thought it was strange."

What was new for Vince was making the transition from bluegrass in small clubs to rock music in big stadiums. "I've always been intrigued by new things, always willing to learn," he said. "Pure Prairie League was a chance for me to step out and perform for lots of people. I don't like being safe with what I do."

Before Vince moved from Kentucky to California, a friend had told him about a woman he would meet. The friend predicted that Vince would fall in love with her and get married.

The Sweethearts of the Rodeo were two sisters from Manhattan Beach, California. Janis and Kristine Oliver were daughters of a Michigan-born housewife of Polish extraction and a California AT&T executive originally from Okmulgee, Oklahoma. When they were five and seven years old, the girls would sing to country music hits. By the age of nine, Janis started playing flat-picking guitar and she became a fan of bluegrass and folk music. She and her sister sang together, with Kristine taking lead and Janis harmonizing. Like many talented youngsters, they found places to sing—in malls, restaurants, and pizza parlors.

In 1973, Janis and Kristine saw the Gram Parsons–inspired Byrds album *Sweetheart of the Rodeo*, and were immediately taken with the cowgirls all dressed up in boots and hats on the cover. They took the name for themselves and incorporated many musical styles in their repertoire, from the Beatles to bluegrass, from Linda Ronstadt to western swing.

All of their high school friends were into rock music, but as Janis said, "We were hooked on country." Their eclectic style was perfect for the times and when they won a talent competition at a Long Beach bluegrass festival, they caught the attention of Emmylou Harris. She invited them to play on shows with her and they also played shows with Poco and Willie Nelson.

One night, at a club in Redondo Beach, the Sweethearts of the Rodeo were opening for Sundance. Janis Oliver and Vince Gill passed each other on the stairway to the stage.

"I caught her eye and she caught my eye, but I don't think she liked my eyes as much as I liked hers," Vince said. "I was pretty smitten with her and asked her out for almost three years, but she would never go out with me. I guess I was a pretty big hillbilly."

"It wasn't right then," Janis said. "What he never mentions is that I had a boyfriend at the time." Vince was three years younger than Janis and she had the impression he wasn't looking for a serious relationship. But they did become good friends.

"She was a beautiful, beautiful girl with these big almond eyes that could break your heart," Vince said.

"There really was an instant attraction," Janis said.

Janis and Kristine sang backup vocals for the song "I'll

Be Damned" on Pure Prairie League's *Firin' Up* album in 1979. Vince wrote that song. Another song he wrote for that album, "Janny Lou," was obviously written for Janis. When Janis and her boyfriend broke up and Vince and his girlfriend also called it quits, they got together. "It didn't take two weeks for us to see it was serious," Vince said.

Vince Gill and Janis Oliver were married in 1980.

> "I'm playing with the greatest musicians in the world, and if the rest of the world didn't know it, it's still OK."
>
> —VINCE GILL

"If it ever comes up that you need a high-harmony singer who plays guitar, please call me." Vince Gill had offered his services to Rodney Crowell after meeting him at the Troubador. For his band, the Cherry Bombs, Crowell had assembled a stellar roster of musicians, including Hank DeVito, Tony Brown, Emory Gordy (all of whom are now top Nashville record producers), and the late drummer Larry London. Around the time that *Firin' Up* was released, Rodney Crowell asked Vince to join the band. Vince said that although he'd wanted this call "for the last five or six years of my musical being," he'd just recorded *Firin' Up* with Pure Prairie League, an album that seemed to have a shot at having some hits. So with regrets he said no.

Vince recorded two more albums with Pure Prairie League. After he left, Gary Burr became lead singer until 1985, when Craig Fuller returned. The group performed their last show on New Year's Eve 1987. Pure Prairie League was a group ahead of its time, and the unique sound it created is reflected in a lot of the music that is popular today. It is worth noting that on the one Pure Prairie League album still available—*The Best of Pure Prairie League*—four of the songs are written by Vince Gill.

But a while later, he decided to join the Cherry Bombs. It was 1982, Janis was pregnant, and Pure Prairie League's sales were slumping. Vince decided to answer Crowell's call.

"People thought I was nuts," he said. "I went from lead singer in a popular band to sideman in a group led by a fledgling writer. But the Cherry Bombs were as good musicians as I'd ever played with in my life. Musically, it was a giant step for me. I had to be on my toes to keep up with them."

At the time, the Cherry Bombs were using three guitarists who floated in and out of the group because they were in such demand by others. Albert Lee was working with Eric Clapton. Richard Bennett was touring with Neil Diamond. And Vince Gill was still working part of the time with Pure Prairie League.

"Each of the three guitarists we used brought something unique to the Cherry Bombs," Tony Brown said, "but the first time Vince toured with us, I was stunned that a person this young had so much talent. I also remember what a cool guy he was," Brown said, "and, above all, I had never heard a voice like this before."

Rosanne Cash also needed a guitar player, so Vince was also playing with her. Rosanne is the daughter of one of the most famous men in country music, Johnny Cash. Her debut album, *Right or Wrong,* in 1979, spawned three hits, including a duet with Bobby Bare called "No Memories Hangin' Round" and the solo "Couldn't Do Nothing Right." In 1979, Rosanne married Rodney Crowell, who produced her next album, *Seven Year Ache*. Released in

1981, it received a Grammy nomination. Rosanne was another important and highly talented music colleague for Vince Gill.

In 1982, Janis and Vince Gill became the proud parents of a daughter whom they named Jenifer. By this time Janis's sister Kristine and her husband, guitarist and singer Leonard Arnold, were also starting a family.

Cherry Bombs keyboardist Tony Brown had gone to Nashville to work for RCA. When he and Vince met up at a Rosanne Cash concert in Houston, Brown offered Vince Gill his first solo record deal. Vince liked that idea.

"When I was in the band, I never seemed to have time to do the session work that I was getting requests for," he said. "Also, I left to pursue a solo career and try to write some better songs."

So, in 1983, Janis and Vince Gill and their daughter, Jenifer, bid farewell to California and said howdy to Tennessee. Kristine and Leonard came to Nashville a year later. Now the emerging group Sweethearts of the Rodeo and RCA's new solo artist Vince Gill would become the newest dream seekers in Music City.

CHAPTER FOUR

Country Dues

"One of the biggest problems we had was convincing Gill he was a star."

—TONY BROWN

Tony Brown's new job as an A&R executive for RCA Nashville was to discover and bring in new acts for the label. In 1983, it had to be a little difficult to figure out what kinds of artists would please the listening public enough to generate the hits a big record company needed.

In the 1970s, all kinds of changes had taken place in the country music business. Rock and pop music were increasing in sales, but country was standing still. The giants who had helped shape the country music industry—people like Johnny Cash, Loretta Lynn, Waylon Jennings, and Conway Twitty—were seeing a decline in sales of their albums. Some Nashville record companies were turning out music that was heavily influenced by pop. Song arrangements featured lush strings and dreamy sounds that were more like Broadway than Nashville's Music Row. Pop country artist Ronnie Milsap was dominating the country charts and racking up lots of CMA awards. Kenny Rogers, going through a pop period in a career that has seen him master every kind of music, was huge. Crystal Gayle, whose material was decidedly pop in spite of the fact that she was Loretta Lynn's younger sister, was the CMA Female Vocalist for two years running.

Nashville was so enamored of pop that from 1977 to 1981, record companies repeatedly refused to sign a cowboy hat–wearing rancher from Texas who was the most authentic country singer to come along in years. They all told George Strait he was *too* country. When Strait was finally given a chance, the record company still wasn't taking any big risks. Strait was given a deal to release one single. Fortunately, that song, "Unwound," was a big hit and the rest is country music history.

How quickly things turned around! By 1982, George Strait was making it big and Nashville suddenly decided to promote the music of artists given the odd name of "new traditionalists." Vince Gill's old pal Ricky Skaggs scored a huge success with his first major label album, *Waitin' for the Sun to Shine*, in 1982, spawning two number-one singles of very traditional music, "Crying My Heart Out Over You" and "I Don't Care." Randy Travis stormed in from North Carolina to sell a million copies of his debut album, *Storms of Life*. An immensely talented young woman from Oklahoma, one Reba McEntire, was so country you could hear the sounds of the western plains in her voice as she was rising to the top. And straight from the hills of Kentucky, the Judds, a mother-daughter duo with a bluegrass-infused sound, were making it big.

Tony Brown's boss at RCA was label president Joe Galante. At the time Vince Gill was signed to RCA, in 1983, Galante was also president of the Country Music Association. One of Galante's missions was to bring Nashville and its musicians, usually treated as music's poor country cousin, into the music mainstream. It was no secret that many of the sophisticated music executives in Los Angeles and New York—where the corporate parents of the Nashville labels were headquartered—thought the music coming out of Nashville was not good enough to compete in the pop world.

Tony Brown knew what a great musician Vince Gill was no matter what kind of music he played. As a musician himself, Brown was interested in Vince Gill for the music. Joe Galante told the press, when announcing Vince's arrival at RCA, "We are extremely proud to have Vince join us. We believe he will play a major role in the future of country music." Given Vince's background in both bluegrass and pop, it was a brilliant comment at a time when Nashville, and in fact the whole music business, was changing directions. Whether country was going pop or pop was going country, Vince Gill was entirely likely to have a big future.

In Nashville, Janis and Vince and Jenifer Gill were getting settled. As Vince told a reporter at the time, "We don't have any furniture, but we've got guitars." It was a start.

Vince was ready to step out in the spotlight as a solo artist. He said it was something he'd always wanted. He'd been offered the opportunity a few times before to quit whatever band he was with and try to make his own record. "And I said, 'No, thank you,' " he explained.

> "I feel like having that patience to wait until I was really ready is going to pay off in the long run."
>
> —VINCE GILL

Before arriving in Nashville, Vince had worked as a musician and vocalist with some very important artists, including Rosanne Cash, Rodney Crowell, Bonnie Raitt, and Emmylou Harris. He had established himself in the world of bluegrass as a consummate master of any string instrument he picked up. He had helped to revitalize Pure Prairie League, writing, recording, and perfoming hits for that great group. Now it was time to see how he would do as a solo artist.

One of Vince's bandmates from the Cherry Bombs was Emory Gordy Jr. "He felt I was going to be the one who could really bridge the gap between pop and country and get rock fans interested in country music," Vince said. Emory Gordy was chosen to produce Vince's first album for RCA. It had to be comforting to Vince to have Gordy with him, since before they even got started, Tony Brown had left RCA to go to work at MCA Nashville, a competing record company.

Turn Me Loose was released in 1984. It was a "mini-album," containing only eight songs, a concept many record companies were experimenting with in the mid-eighties. Vince wrote five of the songs himself. The first single, "Turn Me Loose," one of Vince's, did not score big on radio, but years later remains a favorite country dance song in clubs and a song Vince usually includes in his live concerts. It fulfills the promise heard in "I'll Be Damned," one of the songs Vince wrote and performed with Pure Prairie League. It has a great hook, is more of a rocker than a country or pop song, and would have fit just fine on a Pure Prairie League album. The second single released from the album was "Victim of Life's Circumstances," a song written by Delbert McClinton, one of President Jimmy Carter's favorite artists. It reached the Top 40 but didn't go higher. It's too bad, because the song rocks. Randy Albright, Jim Elliot, and Mark D. Sanders wrote

"Oh Carolina," a great ballad given a great performance by Vince that should have been number one but only squeaked into the Top 40.

The album is a great freshman effort and a sign of the wonderful music to come. Though *Turn Me Loose* didn't set the world on fire, Vince Gill received a big honor in 1984.

The Academy of Country Music, based on the West Coast, was established in 1964 to promote country music around the world. The organization gave out its first awards in 1965. Broadcasts went out locally until 1972, when the show was put into national television syndication. Since 1979, the ACM broadcasts have been associated with Dick Clark Productions. Academy members vote for awards in eleven major categories.

On May 6, 1984, the Academy of Country Music named Vince Gill the top New Male Vocalist. It was a sweet victory. "It means a lot," Vince said. "It lets you know that somebody's hearing what you're doing."

Vince Gill's Academy of Country Music Awards

1984 New Male Vocalist of the Year

1992 Song of the Year for "I Still Believe in You"

1992 Top Male Vocalist of the Year

1993 Top Male Vocalist of the Year

His solo career may have been moving slowly, but Vince was still playing a lot of music. There are recording sessions going on every day in the multitude of recording studios that line Nashville's Music Row. Even artists who have their own bands, which play with them in concerts, generally turn to studio musicians, also known as session players, when it comes to recording their albums. There's a big difference between playing a live concert and making a record. On stage you can cut loose, have fun, and not worry whether every note will withstand the test of time. It doesn't have to. But in the studio, a precise level of polished playing is required. Some of the best musicians in Nashville rarely, if ever, see a stage. They can listen to a demo a few times, read charts prepared by producers, and play the music exactly the way the artist and producer want it to be heard. And they can do it fast. Studio time costs money. Producers, and the record companies and artists who foot the bills for recording, need players and singers who can deliver the goods.

It didn't take Nashville long to figure out that Vince Gill was one of those players. His guitar playing was so superior that he was in high demand as a session player. His voice was also an asset to any artist who asked him to do backup vocals. "I could play," he said, "but they usually got me for my singing." During the 1980s in Nashville, Vince played and sang for everyone from Conway Twitty to Kim Carnes, from Lee Greenwood to Bonnie Raitt. He says he never felt jealous of the artists who became successful before he did. He felt that getting to play, write, and record with these artists was a huge opportunity. "I think what it's taught me more than anything else is to have an open mind and to be receptive and willing to learn something from every situation," he said. "Pull the good stuff out of everything you can, and use it." Altogether, during the 1980s, he lent his music skills to more than a hundred artists. One of these was Patty Loveless.

A genuine coal miner's daughter from Beecher Holler, Kentucky, Patty Loveless grew up on bluegrass and traditional country. When she was only fourteen, she came to Nashville with a catalog of thirty songs she had written. That got the attention of Porter Wagoner and his singing partner, Dolly Parton. It was Patty's high lonesome voice, one that lends itself to songs of heartbreak and love, that got her a job as the featured singer with the Wilburn Brothers while she was still in high school. Then she got married and went to live in North Carolina, where she worked with a variety of bands.

Loveless returned to Nashville in 1983, the same year Vince Gill hit town. Her demo tape found its way to Tony Brown at MCA Records and he signed her to a deal. When Vince Gill sang on her debut album, *Patty Loveless*, it was the first blending of their two amazing voices.

> "I felt like I've made it big ever since I left home. I have always been able to support myself with music and get the rent paid and the family fed."
>
> —VINCE GILL

Vince worked on his songwriting in Nashville—the town that can easily be considered the songwriting capital of the world. As a songwriter, he naturally gravitated toward the Bluebird Cafe.

A small and fairly ordinary-looking little place in one of the many small shopping centers that line Hillsboro Pike in Nashville, the Bluebird is the most important stop in

Music City for aspiring songwriters. Showcases are held several times a week where singers try out their songs before an audience that can include top producers and record company executives, always on the lookout for new talent. Established writers also love to play there, either to try out new material or simply to play for people they know truly love to hear the music.

Vince said he realized he was known in certain situations as a player and in others as a performer. "I wanted my songwriting to catch up, to be that good. Of the things that I did, I felt that was lacking." Challenged, even if it was only by himself, Vince was developing and improving his songwriting all the time. He had songs recorded by Rosanne Cash, Anne Murray, and Crystal Gayle, among others.

After *Turn Me Loose*, Vince took a year off to concentrate on his songwriting. He felt it was easier for him to sing songs he'd written himself. By this time, other songwriters were submitting their compositions for Vince to use on his albums, but for the most part he felt "you've got to sing about things you know to make it believable." The musicians he respected the most—like Willie Nelson, Rodney Crowell, Emmylou Harris, and Merle Haggard—wrote most of their own material and had developed their own style.

"Respect is more important to me than anything," he said. "In twenty years I want people to say, 'I want to be like Vince Gill,' like I say now, 'I want to be like Merle Haggard.' He's brilliant. He did it his way, he stood up there, wrote those songs and has so much character. I want people to feel that way about me."

In November 1985, while opening a show at Veterans Memorial in Columbus, Ohio, for T. G. Sheppard, Vince told a reporter, "I feel like now I'm writing better songs. That's the bottom line. Once the songs are good, it doesn't matter what format or style it is. It's still a good song."

Format and style were big words in Nashville. When Vince came to town, many people perceived him as a pop singer because of his stint with Pure Prairie League. But Vince didn't see himself that way. "I wasn't as skilled or as knowledgeable in pop music as I was in country," he said. "When it came time to make my own records, pop music wasn't like me. I've always wanted to be a country singer." But Vince recognized that starting a country career was like starting over.

He was frustrated, as many artists were, with all the categorizing of music into different formats. Some people called Vince's music "modern-oriented country music." He felt that his music had both traditional country roots and some modern influences.

In 1985, RCA released its second Vince Gill album, entitled *The Things That Matter*. From the start it was clear that this album would do better than *Turn Me Loose*. Vince had another Top 40 hit with a song he'd written entitled "True Love." It pays homage to the great Roy Orbison in the vocal styling. He broke into the Top 10 with "If It Weren't for Him," a duet with Rosanne Cash that the two had written together. The song had originally been intended as a cut on *Turn Me Loose*, but legal hassles between Rosanne's and Vince's record companies had delayed its release. (Vince also played and sang vocals on almost every song on Rosanne's very successful *Rhythm and Romance* album released in 1985.) A song he'd written with Rodney Crowell and Guy Clark, two great Texas songwriters, "Oklahoma Borderline," also hit the Top 10.

Most important, he was having fun. Throughout that year, he opened a lot of shows for Ricky Skaggs. When he played at the Ingham County Fair near Lansing, Michigan, he said, "It's the last show of my tour and we're going to have a ball." He said he loved playing outdoors at fairs. "Fairgrounds are a lot of fun. You get to eat corndogs and hang out on the rides."

He may have been having fun, but Vince Gill's career was moving slowly. "I don't mind not being an overnight success," he said on one occasion. "My records aren't safe and some country deejays hesitate to play new artists. They want to stick to Kenny and Dolly and Alabama. I've been a little frustrated that some of my singles weren't bigger hits, but each single has done better than the last one."

> "They put the country label on it because it comes from Nashville and I come from Oklahoma. It would be nice if people got away from labels. Branding the music tends to limit it."
>   —VINCE GILL

Country radio was playing Vince Gill a little but pop radio wasn't, even though he'd had a pop hit or two as the lead singer with Pure Prairie League. Once a song or artist is presented as being in one category, the other categories of radio tend to stay away. Artists aren't the only ones who miss out when this happens. People who like all kinds of music have to keep changing stations to hear the full gamut of what's out there at any given time. "I'd like to break down the barriers that have people judging before they've heard," Vince said. "I know I can make a good pop record, a record that's not off the beaten path for country, too. It still comes down to great music and the songs themselves."

Vince wanted his albums to be filled with great songs. He didn't agree with the current trend in Nashville to place so much emphasis on a few hit singles, paying less attention to the rest of the songs on the album. "I want to write and perform ten hits and get them heard," he said. He pointed out that this was what Michael Jackson, Cyndi Lauper, and other pop artists of the mid-1980s were doing. "They make albums full of hits and that's the way you have to go today: Make an album so deep and so good, people will have to buy it."

He expressed a fondness for rockers like Bruce Springsteen and John Fogerty. "I've said all along that I would keep an honesty in my music. It's like Springsteen. He's giving all he's got and it's coming from the heart." Vince was glad to see John Fogerty, of Creedence Clearwater Revival, coming back with a solo career. "It made me say there's hope after all. There's no reason why someone who listens to Don Henley can't like me and vice versa. There're so many acts that I draw from."

Vince was pretty clear about what kind of country act he wanted to be. "You ask any rock and roller what his favorite country act is," Vince said, "and he'll say either Merle Haggard or George Jones, because they're classic songwriters and singers who don't follow trends."

Vince didn't want to follow trends. Like most musicians, he wanted the music to be the priority.

"There was an attitude in Nashville several years ago that said you made records a certain way. It took Waylon [Jennings] and Willie [Nelson] coming in and saying 'No you don't' to change that. Nashville is more open-minded now. I'm not doing anything that's so radical that country people can't enjoy it because my roots are entrenched in country music." It was getting a little discouraging.

> "Sometimes you just sit there and wonder if you're ever going to be a platinum act or a gold act like all these other people. After a while you start to think, 'Well, maybe this is where I settle in. This is where I wind up.' "
>
> —VINCE GILL

The annual Wrangler Country Showdown calls itself the world's largest country music talent contest. Each year more than 150,000 hopeful artists and groups go through several rounds of competition to see if anyone thinks they're good enough to be heard. In 1985, after having taken a break from their careers to get settled in Nashville, Janis Gill and Kristine Arnold, the Sweethearts of the Rodeo, reached the semifinals and finals and became the Showdown's national winners. Vince had believed in his wife's talents all along and had brought a tape to Columbia Records. By the time the Sweethearts won the Wrangler Country Showdown, Columbia had signed them to a recording contract.

In 1986, their first album, entitled *Sweethearts of the Rodeo*, was released. Like Vince's *Turn Me Loose*, it was an eight-song mini-album. At the time, Janis Gill was asked what kind of music the Sweethearts were making. "Imagine if the Everly Brothers were female and making records in 1986," she said. "That's what we sound like." In fact, their first single, "Hey Doll Baby," an obscure Everly Brothers tune, became a Top 20 country hit. It was followed by another song that hit the Top 10, Foster and

Lloyd's "Since I Found You." By the end of 1986, the Sweethearts had their third and biggest hit, "Midnight Girl/Sunset Town," that reached the Top 5. "Chains of Gold" and "Gotta Get Away" also made it to the Top 10. It was a stunning debut for a new group—five hits from an eight-song album. One of Janis's biggest fans was her husband. He was "thrilled and proud," he said.

Was it difficult that Janis was making it big before he did? "It's not a surprise because we both have wanted it," Vince said. "There isn't time for us to be competing and be jealous of each other or any of that kind of stuff. It's not worth it." Vince said the hardest part for them was the long separations when one or both were on the road.

The Gills weren't all that different from a lot of working couples. The baby-boom generation was creating another sea change in American life: two-career couples with young children. Whether two jobs came about out of financial necessity or from the fact that women were coming to believe that their career ambitions were as important as men's, the reality was the same. Janis told *People* magazine that because her career took off so quickly, she was being pulled in a million different directions and that "it was tough getting into the rhythm and rhyme of a life like that."

Vince admitted that at times it was hard for him that Janis made it first. But he didn't begrudge her success. He just wanted to make it, too.

Janis said, "I've always been Vince's greatest fan and I knew how much he deserved a shot." She said she felt guilty about making it, on top of feeling guilty about not being around as much as she wanted to for her daughter. "But it's nobody's fault," she said. "I just happened to get my break first."

When they could, Janis and Vince were taking turns going out on the road so that one of them could be home with Jenny. "Jenny's not blown away if she sees Mom and Dad on TV anymore," Vince said. "She's got a pretty level head on her shoulders."

One of the nice things Vince was able to do while staying home with Jenny was to get involved in her school. When there was no money in the school budget for an art teacher, he and other parents helped raise some. Vince was quick to say that he's not a very political person and he didn't feel that being a singer gave him the right to stand on a soapbox and yell his views. "But creativity is an important part of one's life, not just socially but spiritually," he said.

> "I still approach it from that artistic and creative side. All the sales and other parts of it are secondary. That's the way it has to be if you're going to call yourself an artist."
>
> —VINCE GILL

In 1986, RCA and Vince Gill were preparing for their third album together. The company still believed in him. The first two albums had been well received by both music critics and the industry even if the sales numbers hadn't been huge. Maybe the third time around would be the charm.

"This was a real pivotal record for me," Vince said. "This one needed to be a lot bigger and a lot better. I took a lot of time writing this record."

One idea was to bring in a different producer. West Coast producer Richard Landis, came up with some interesting studio ideas for Vince's songs. Changing producers is never easy for an artist, and at first Vince said he thought, "Oh my God, we're going to kill each other." Vince asked around about Landis and was told he was kind of outspoken and liked things his way. Landis called him up and said, "Hey, I hear around town that you think I'm a tyrant." Vince told him, "That doesn't mean you're a bad guy. You can be a tyrant all day long if you're right, but I can be just as much of a tyrant back if I think you're wrong." In the end, Vince said, "We had a really neat relationship and it worked out great. I think everyone expected a slick pop record because Richard makes good, slick records, but we both had our ideas and it worked."

Vince considered his upcoming third album his best chance yet. "Back in 1984," he said, "there wasn't the emphasis on new music in country as there is today. Only two new artists reached the Top 10 that year. Now there are a lot more."

Things were broadening a bit in country radio by the time the new album was released in 1987. Pop-sounding songs could be played right after something traditional by, say, George Strait or Ricky Skaggs. That was good. Without radio play, artists wanting hits could pack up their guitars and go home.

Vince's new album was called *The Way Back Home*. He played most of the music himself and wrote or co-wrote seven of the nine tunes. "I'm really proud of this album as far as the lyrical growth is concerned," he said. "I'm doing handstands right now because everybody was saying, 'Well, are we gonna get another handful of Vince's sad songs?' " Vince decided not to let his ego get in the way and instead allowed producer Richard Landis and RCA's A&R staff to select the material.

"Cinderella," written by Reed Nielsen, was the first

single from the album. "It's kind of new wave, hillbilly/ bluegrass music in a way," Vince said. "We recorded it and then started putting all the mandolin and banjo on it." This was the first album where Vince played banjo, mandolin, and Dobro, the instruments he'd used so often in his bluegrass days. "There are things on this album that are really different," he said, "but it has a real cohesiveness. Richard has a real concept of boundaries."

Vince said "Cinderella" reminded him of a cross between Bill Monroe and the Beatles. In the song, the singer scolds his friend for trying to force his girlfriend to be Cinderella. He says he'll take the girl and treat her like a real person if the friend doesn't change his ways. The song made it into the Top 5 and the album was off to a great start.

The title track, "The Way Back Home," is a sensitive ballad with a relaxed pace, a truly touching song about the plight of missing children. Vince had never written about an important issue like that and said it was his favorite song of all those he'd written so far in his career. The song came about after Vince heard about a "to whom it may concern" letter from a woman to his record company suggesting that some of the artists take the time to write about the problem. "It's not preachy," Vince said. "All it is doing is saying, 'If you've got a minute, look out for something weird.' I have a daughter and I can't tell you what it does to me when she is not exactly where I think she is sometimes."

Fans of one of rock and roll's earliest innovators, Buddy Holly, found a new, very country arrangement of his classic "It Doesn't Matter Anymore," written by another icon, Paul Anka. On "Let's Do Something," written by Vince and Reed Nielsen, the incomparable Bonnie Raitt joins Vince for some good-time rocking. "Baby, That's Tough" is a good-natured reflection of the male backlash at women's liberation.

One reviewer said that the range of the album's contents was broad, with a nice variety in song themes. Another said the songs showcased Vince's talents as a songwriter and musician. Yet another said the magic words: The album showed Vince had what it takes to make it in country.

Like many artists, Vince was struggling with balancing his desire to make it big and his devotion to making music he believed in. "I don't knock commercialism," he said. People were always talking about all the great music that doesn't get made because of commercial concerns, but Vince felt the really good stuff could still get out there. "Bluegrass is great," he said, "but it's never going to sell millions of records." That shouldn't be the criteria of success, he felt, but unfortunately, if you were going to be in the record business, that's what you lived and died by.

> "If I'm going to make it in this business, I can't be Mr. Eclectic Hipster."
>
> —VINCE GILL

Janis Gill and Kristine Arnold—the Sweethearts of the Rodeo—sang some backup vocals on *The Way Back Home*. Vince also made a guest appearance, along with his good friend Rodney Crowell, on the Sweethearts' second album on the Everly Brothers' tune "So Sad to Watch Good Love Go Bad." The Sweethearts were still tearing up the charts. Vince was happy for them.

One of the songs on *The Way Back Home* was "Everybody's Sweetheart," an ode to being in love with someone who's famous and on the road. Vince said he liked adding a sense of humor to his record making because "I'm nuts in real life." He said life shouldn't be taken so seriously. "It's obviously about Janis," he said. "It's like I'm getting a taste of my own medicine. She's going away and that's cool. I'm really proud of her."

The personal note in the song was more of an inside joke, Vince felt. "Let's not kid ourselves—we're not the Beatles and Tina Turner. In the industry, everybody knows, but a lot of people in the world don't know that Janis and I are married."

Another song on *The Way Back Home* was also about Janis and Vince. "Reed Nielsen had started 'The Radio' and it made me think of Janis and the traveling," Vince said. "That's the only time I ever hear her, on the radio. It's a lonely song, but it's not a feel-sorry-for-yourself song. It says that's the price you pay for the life you choose."

On other records, Vince said, he had started second-guessing what he thought the music should be instead of doing what he knew it should be. He felt more confident in *The Way Back Home*. "It's doing better than anything else ever has."

"Why isn't writer/singer/multiinstrumentalist Vince Gill a star yet?"

—*Nashville Banner*

The Way Back Home sold twice as many copies as *The Things That Matter*. But real commercial success wasn't yet in hand for Vince. "Sure, I get frustrated," he said. "I don't know why my records haven't sold more, really I don't. I have the respect of my peers, which is worth a lot. The record company is as frustrated as I am about the situation."

He knew that if he really worried about it all, it wouldn't be worth the ulcers he would get. Yet he did start looking ahead. The good news was that he never stopped working on the music he loved.

In the mid-eighties, he joined forces with Emmylou Harris and other artists on her latest project. Since the late seventies, Emmylou had been carving out an impressive career as a fine musician and a magnificent singer. Her album *Elite Hotel*, released in 1975 after *Pieces of the Sky* had made her a star, spawned three Top 5 singles, including a remake of the Patsy Cline classic "Sweet Dreams." *Quarter Moon in a Ten Cent Town* in 1978 gave the world such Top 10 hits as "Two More Bottles of Wine," "To Daddy," and "Easy From Now On." Her Hot Band was considered the ultimate finishing school for musicians of all kinds. Though true commercial success in the sense it was being defined in the 1980s wouldn't come to Emmylou Harris, she continued to put out albums of startling originality and steller performances. Songs like "Boulder to Birmingham" and "Born to Run" are two of the hits people love from Emmylou. In 1987 she released *Trio* (with Linda Ronstadt and Dolly Parton) in which three of the greatest voices ever created came together. Four songs—"To Know Him Is to Love Him," "Telling Me Lies," "Those Memories of You," and "Wildflowers"— were Top 10 hits.

The project that brought Vince Gill, picker/singer Carl Jackson, and bassist, producer, and former Cherry Bombs member Emory Gordy Jr. together with Emmylou was the *Angel Band* album, a collection of gospel standards with acoustic accompaniments, released in 1987. Vince said making the album was as much fun as he'd ever had doing music. "She always has been a pioneer, doing things she cared about," he said of Emmylou. "The four of us just got together for fun, and Emmylou's husband had a little studio in the house." The album was recorded live in one take. *Angel Band*, with the voices of Vince Gill and Emmylou Harris, was a gorgeous blending of harmony that, combined with the deep lyrics of the songs, created a truly memorable listening experience. "We sat around in a circle and had fun," Vince said. "I don't get to do that stuff enough. Remember, I'm an old bluegrasser."

Vince loved to work with his friends. "It's great to surround yourself with people who are so much better than you," he said graciously. "It gives you something to try to achieve."

The *Angel Band* experience is something Vince describes as "one of my proudest moments." While making that album, Vince had turned down a commercial jingle session that conflicted with the schedule. It turned out to have been a hugely lucrative beer commercial. But Vince was busy doing something else, for the music.

The angels must have been watching over Vince and his band when, in the winter of 1987–88, their tour bus slid on an icy freeway off-ramp outside of Denver and crashed into an eighteen-wheel semi-rig truck. The bus was demolished but the occupants were not injured. The truck, it seems, saved them—if the bus hadn't hit it, it would have gone over an embankment.

Mark Knopfler of Dire Straits had heard Vince singing on the Patty Loveless album and asked everyone he met, "Who is that singer?"

Once Knopfler found out—and also heard Vince's guitar playing—he asked him to join Dire Straits for their upcoming world tour. Vince thought about it and even played guitar on the new Dire Straits album, but decided against joining the group as a regular member.

He said he was "an extra-large fan" of Dire Straits and was flattered to be asked. "But I told Mark I had invested too much time in country music to change," he said. "I didn't know if the country career was going to pan out, but it's where my heart is and where I wanted to stay."

> "Someone like Vince puts you in your place if you think you're hot stuff. Puts me in my place. He writes, sings on all the best records in Nashville, plays guitar like a god, of course, and then can do it on mandolin or something else."
> —MARK KNOPFLER

Knopfler also pointed out what a great golfer Vince was. Should he have become a professional golfer instead of a professional musician? At times, perhaps, he felt that way. Other artists were hitting it big and Vince wasn't really hitting it yet at all. "A lot of people figured I was done. Nothing major had happened and people started losing enthusiasm." Vince said he never doubted he had a hit in him. It was just hard trying to find it. He knew he was pretty good. He felt like he belonged in the music business. He knew he could play and sing. "I don't mean that egotistically," he said. "My ears tell me that I have some talent. And I love it. I mean music is the greatest thing in my life."

He had no regrets. "I'd have done it no matter what, no matter where I wound up on this totem pole of popularity." Vince didn't care if he was on the records as a harmony singer or as a guitar player. "As long as I got to be on 'em, it kind of felt good to me, just to be a part of it." He recognized he'd been very lucky. He'd already played more music in fourteen years than some musicians play in a lifetime. The writing and the session work saw to that. He didn't have to come to Nashville, as so many musicians had, and work as a waiter in the Waffle House or do construction or other jobs that were perfectly respectable but took a lot of time away from the goal of making music.

He did feel bad that there were so many great players who wanted to work with him but whom he couldn't keep around because he didn't have enough work for them.

For the next album, Vince decided he was going to stop thinking so much and just do what felt right to him. "It's almost a curse that I can play so many different kinds of music," he said, "but I can and I don't want to curb that any more."

In the middle of planning Vince's fourth album at RCA, label president Joe Galante suggested he not record any of his own songs. Vince had a problem with that. He knew some people felt his lack of success was because he recorded his own songs. Others thought he just hadn't found the right record yet. Everyone knew he was great. Maybe the timing wasn't right. Later, Vince felt the slow road to success had given him a lot of time to hang out, watch the business, and learn a lot of good things. It's just that in 1988, he hadn't gone far enough down that road to appreciate the slow times.

"I was satisfied at RCA. I have no animosity toward them," he said. "They honestly did what they felt was right. My hat's off to them for as much effort as they put out." Vince said he felt fortunate that everybody had stuck with him and still believed in him enough to want to continue to make records.

But in the end, Vince Gill and Joe Galante decided they would probably never agree on what to do, so Gill suggested it was time for him to leave RCA. He said that Galante, who was "a friend," and RCA, "who had done their best for me," agreed.

Tony Brown was now a major force at MCA Records in Nashville. When Vince left RCA, Tony Brown signed him to MCA. He would also become Vince Gill's record producer.

CHAPTER FIVE

Striking Gold

"I enjoy it all. What I've always wanted, though,
is a hit record, a real whopper."

—VINCE GILL

When Vince Gill moved from RCA to MCA Records,
he was joining a record company that had already proven
its success in taking country artists to the top. His label-
mates included some of the giants, like George Strait and
Reba McEntire. But the most important person at MCA as
far as Vince was concerned was Tony Brown, who had
signed Vince to his recording contract at RCA but had left
the company before he and Vince could work together.

"The chance to work with Tony Brown was something I
always wanted," Vince said. "We kinda got started about
the same time. It is critical to find the right producer."

It is also critical to make a stand as to the kind of music
you're going to play. Much as many musicians are frustrated by the strict categorization of types of music, it is a
reality of the business. Up to now, Vince Gill had been ex-
ploring the many different kinds of music that captured his
imagination as an artist. Now he was ready to declare himself country all the way. "It eventually comes to the point
where you ask yourself what do you do best," he said. He

knew it was time to go with his strongest suit, with the kind of music he loved and that he knew would also move audiences the most.

In September 1988, Vince Gill opened a show for that great, sexy-voiced, fun-loving lady of country Tanya Tucker. He got great reviews for his solo performance, which featured songs he said would be part of his next album. He said he did not set particular goals in music because, if he achieved them, he might quit trying to do more. "The sky's the limit in this profession," he said.

But he did give a hint as to what might come in the future from the guy who was rapidly becoming one of the best-loved voices in music. "I'm going back to my roots," he said. "I've tried to get away from my roots by blending a mix of pop and country. It really didn't work for me and I'm going back to country."

In 1989, MCA released its first Vince Gill album. It was called *When I Call Your Name* and was unlike any of his previous albums in a number of ways.

Tony Brown produced the album and, as is his style, gave Vince a great deal of creative control. "When you have an artist like Vince," he said, "the producer is nothing more than a coach or conductor."

Vince wrote or co-wrote seven of the songs on the album. He said he enjoyed the collaborative songwriting process. "I could write songs by myself," he said, "but I don't. It's not as much fun as writing with someone else. . . . I really like being around people." He felt the album represented the best collection of songs he'd ever written. They covered a wide range of styles that could all be called country. It was in some ways an experiment to see which

style of country songs from Vince Gill people would gravi-
tate toward the most.

Vince said that this album meant a lot to him because it
was really country. "For a while, I didn't know that that
was what I wanted to do. But now, looking back, you learn
things from what you've done the last four or five years.
I'm finally learning the place I ought to be and enjoying it."

When the album was done, Vince joked that he was
looking forward to "touring and just watching my record
leap up the charts." There was a wish in that comment—a
wish that would come true.

With his old friend Rosanne Cash, Vince wrote "Never
Alone," the song that opens the album. Very evocative of
1970s pop music, it was nevertheless thoroughly country.
The story in the song is filled with a generosity of spirit.
Even as a man is hearing his girlfriend say good-bye to
him, he promises her she'll never be alone. Great rhythm
guitar serves as a wonderful background for Vince Gill's
own excellent lead guitar playing. It was the first single released to radio and signaled to country radio that a new
star was on the horizon. Fans responded well and the song
made the Top 20 on radio play charts.

On that song, Vince sang his own background vocals.
On the other songs, he used a lot of different vocalists for
background. It made a big difference in his sound. "I sang
the background on all my other records, and the reason I
did it is because I'm lazy," he said with a chuckle. "It's
easy to do. It doesn't cost anything more. But when you do
that, there's only one vocal character on the album."

On "Sight for Sore Eyes," which Vince co-wrote with
Guy Clark, Kathie Baillie of Baillie and the Boys sang
backup. The lovely sentiment is about the importance of
having someone in your life who serves as a beacon of

light during times of pain. Harry Stinson and Billy Thomas provide background vocals, along with Vince, on "Oh Girl (You Know Where to Find Me)," a song with a smooth melody and an r&b rhythm that Vince wrote on his own. Taking the great Temptations songs and other Motown hits to the country, Vince Gill proves he's got as much soul as any singer of our times. Though the electric guitar and bass throughout the song are evocative of Motown, the guitar solo is done with an acoustic guitar. It is pure country and pure Vince. Other guest vocalists on *When I Call Your Name* include Patty Loveless, Emmylou Harris, and Herb Pedersen from the Desert Rose Band.

> "I got 'em because I wanted to get the best I could get. These people are my friends and I don't mind stacking the deck."
>
> —VINCE GILL

But even with all the different background vocals, what really stood out on *When I Call Your Name* was Vince Gill's own voice. Prior albums had been mixed to give the instruments more weight, because for a long time Vince had been hesitant to showcase his voice. Part of this was due to his shyness about his singing, but it was mostly due to his orientation as a musician and guitarist. With this new album, he and Brown decided to put the vocals right up front, giving listeners a surprise as they discovered Vince's amazing singing power. Vince told reporters, "I wanted to do something really country that showcased my voice."

The songs on *When I Call Your Name* range from western swing to a bluegrass-tinged waltz, from contemporary ballads to upbeat Buck Owens–influenced sounds.

The range of Vince's talents shines through because he wasn't afraid to let himself put so many different types of music on one album. Before, he said, he was afraid he would appear unfocused as an artist by including such a range of material.

The *Pittsburgh Press* summed up what many critics had to say about Vince's first major country album. "Showcases veteran Vince Gill as the multitalented artist he is . . . his songwriting, instrumental ability and tenor voice. The album is also the key to mainstream success in country music."

Proving that he could find great songs as well as write them, Vince recorded a few gems. "We Won't Dance," written by Greg Trooper, includes background vocals by Anthony Crawford. "We Could Have Been," by Don Cook (who has written a lot of hits for Brooks & Dunn, among others) and John Barlow Jarvis features background vocals by Vince and Kathy Baillie. On "Rita Ballou" by Guy Clark, Vince's old friend, Emmylou Harris sang background vocals. In choosing these songs for this critically important first MCA album, Vince said he was glad he could operate on the theory of finding good songs and recording them the way they were meant to be recorded. With his own incredible vocal treatment, other great background vocals, and the arrangements that bring country and pop close together, the songs are beautiful additions to the album.

"Oklahoma Swing" was written with Tim DuBois. It was a duet that Vince recorded with another Oklahoma native, the one and only Reba McEntire. There's a great lead guitar solo that transitions into the final solo by the laptop steel guitar. Although it went to number four in radio play, there were many stations that wouldn't play it at all because it was in the western swing style. Vince was unhappy that so many stations wouldn't touch this important early form of country music pioneered by Bob Wills and His Texas Playboys. He did joke, "I'm pretty sure it will be a big hit in Oklahoma anyhow. I don't know about the rest of the world." That was a good bet since all the artists involved—Vince Gill, Tim DuBois, and Reba McEntire—were native Oklahomans.

Another song for the Oklahoma crowd was "Ridin' the Rodeo," a hard-edged song about life on the road that Vince wrote with the acclaimed songwriter Kostas. Herb Pedersen sang background vocals.

The one song on the album Vince felt most strongly about was the title cut. He co-wrote "When I Call Your Name" with Tim DuBois.

> "It's the kind of song that gave me goose bumps. I felt it was going to be a hit. I was confident that if this was not a hit, then I could throw my hands up and say I don't have a clue to what is."
>
> —VINCE GILL

The song tells the story of a man who comes home from work only to discover that his mate has left him. No one is answering when he calls out her name. The piano was in the style of Floyd Cramer, who is to country piano what George Jones is to country singing, and the pedal steel playing, by renowned session player Paul Franklin, make the song as country as biscuits and gravy. Patty Loveless's background vocals only add to the plaintive, heartbreaking sound. The song can make you picture the farmhouse with the table and the note on it, so real is its description, so true is its feeling. Tony Brown didn't understand what Vince was going for at first by having Patty Loveless on background, according to Vince, but he went wild after he heard it. "The music has an old gospel feel to it," Vince said, "and the Patty Loveless harmony makes it very bluegrass. And it's sadder than a one-car funeral."

Every country radio station in America played "When I Call Your Name" when it was released in 1990. The song became a number-one single and suddenly, with one song, Vince Gill's musical career was sent into the stratosphere. People were calling the song an instant classic. The success was gratifying after wondering for years if he really had what it took to be a top singer/songwriter.

"Some people were ready to put my foot on a banana peel and give me a shove," he said. "To be around as long as I've been and then have this major hit—it was a major, major blessing."

He didn't want to spend a lot of time analyzing the song and why it was a hit, although he did agree that there were many elements that drew people to "When I Call Your Name," including the gospel-style piano and the crying steel guitar. "It just has all the elements of real, hard-core country music," he said. "I just think I made the right record at the right time."

Vince had another thrill with "When I Call Your Name." He sang it in the presence of Roy Acuff, a grand old master of country music, and watched a tear come to Acuff's eye. A photo was taken of the event, and after Acuff's death in 1992, Vince said that photo was one of his prized possessions.

The good Oklahoma common sense that had guided Vince Gill so far in his life was still in place when he looked at the change in his status with the success of "When I Call

Your Name." He compared himself to Bonnie Raitt. Raitt was a great singer and performer who worked for years making superb records to excellent critical acclaim before having her first huge commercial hit with "Let's Give Them Something to Talk About." Though many artists hit it big with their debut efforts, and though our fast-paced media age seems to expect that, Vince Gill and real artists like him take some time to grow.

"A lot of people think you have to be number one or you're not happy," he said. He'd told himself back in the eighties that making some pretty good records that didn't sell a lot of copies was better than selling several million and not liking what you're doing. Now he had the best of both worlds.

Still, he was philosophical. "I never think about why it didn't happen those seven years. Because it doesn't matter in a sense. I figure that if it had happened then, then my career'd be over now, and I wouldn't be having any fun now."

" 'When I Call Your Name' is a return to the melodic and emotional spirit of Vince Gill's music's early days in Oklahoma when he played and sang bluegrass music."
                              —JACK HURST, *Chicago Tribune*

The success of the single and the album changed everything on the road for Vince Gill. Suddenly there were more gigs for more money in better places. Offers poured in to open shows for bigger acts. There was a lot more airplay of other songs from *When I Call Your Name*. And, of course, the video—Vince's first—showed country television viewers the man behind the songs they were coming to love.

The video opens with a pianist's hands playing the song's touching intro. Then we see Vince in an empty house, its brightly lit walls and windows an eerie contrast to the sadness within. There are wonderful close-ups and then longer shots of Vince looking out the window, as somber and serious as the song sounds. In the background is a woman looking lonely, a woman that Vince doesn't see in the video. There is no guitar in sight, this being a look at Vince Gill the singer. A close-up of the pedal steel guitar reminds us of the big part that instrument plays in this song. Watching the video, as good as it is, you begin to realize that Vince's songs don't need videos. The lyrics and music are so vivid, they hark back to the days before videos, the days when listeners could picture in their minds the stories and characters in the songs.

One day Vince and his road crew were talking about whether they could afford to add a few more guys. They realized that just a few months earlier they couldn't have even had that conversation.

"About the time 'When I Call Your Name' started flying and doing great things," Vince said, "we pulled into this honky tonk where we were booked. We couldn't find a parking place. It was that way from the summer on. Everywhere we went there was a big crowd."

Someone asked him what had made "When I Call Your Name" click as a hit song. "I wish I knew," Vince said. "I would bottle it up and do it every time."

At one amusement park the crowd was going crazy for Vince Gill. They stood up and moved toward the stage, and he could see people singing all the words and some of them crying. "The response was so genuine and so overwhelming that I was shocked," Vince said. "That had never happened to me in my whole life. I started crying myself."

One fan was in tears when he approached Vince to tell him how much the song meant to him. His own wife had taken their children and left behind only a note. Other fans interpreted the meaning of the song to be about the death of a loved one, something Vince had never intended. It showed he was the best kind of songwriter, one who could appeal to different people in different ways, and whose lyrics were universal enough to become personal, personal enough to become universal.

Even with his success, Vince Gill wasn't about to become an arrogant superstar. Though he was able to buy some better transportation than he'd had before for going on the road, he still wanted to be just another guy in the band. "I travel with the band on the bus and everybody gets to play and has a good time playing," he said. "It's not at all me the big star and you guys sit in the back and just back me up. We really do have a lot of fun out there."

Performing live in front of fans was something Vince Gill had been doing all his life. In October 1990, he had the chance to perform "When I Call Your Name" before a television audience of millions—and before all of the most important people in the country music business, assembled in the Grand Ole Opry for the most important annual event in the business, the Country Music Association Awards.

> "I was cool all day at rehearsals and prior to the show. I never considered the thought of winning."
>
> —VINCE GILL

Before the Country Music Association announces its nominees each year, all of Nashville is abuzz with anticipation. The CMA was the first trade organization formed to promote a specific type of music. Founded in 1958, it originally consisted of only 233 members. Today it has more than 7,000 organizational and individual members in thirty-one countries. The CMA Awards, inaugurated in 1967, are presented annually in twelve categories to outstanding country artists. Voted on by the members themselves, including songwriters, musicians, artists, record executives, and others directly involved in the day-to-day creation and promotion of country music, these awards are the most prestigious of all the awards given in the field.

Among the nominees for Single of the Year—an award that goes to the artist, whereas Song of the Year goes to the songwriter—was "When I Call Your Name." Songs by Kathy Mattea, Clint Black, and Garth Brooks were also among the nominees.

Vince Gill and Patty Loveless sang their hearts out on "When I Call Your Name" for an audience of people who came into the Opry House that night already loving them. Each had contributed so much to country music and to the Nashville music scene. Patty had scored two number-one hits, "Timber, I'm Falling in Love" and "Chairs," from her 1988 album, *Honky Tonk Angel*. And Vince had just gotten the big breakthrough everyone knew he'd deserved for years. It was a magical moment. The crowd rewarded them with a heartfelt standing ovation.

"When the entire country music world stood up and applauded," Vince said, "that was the best feeling."

Many people in the audience were truly rooting for Vince to win. Obviously, many of them had put their votes where their hearts were. The envelope was opened and "When I Call Your Name" won Single of the Year. It was time for another standing ovation.

"Better than winning Single of the Year was the reaction of the people in the crowd that night," Vince said. "For once it was like nobody cared what label it was that won the award. Competition was thrown out the window. It was so heartwarming to see that kind of response."

Right after the CMA Awards, Vince took to the road again. In October he played at the L. C. Walker Arena in Muskegon, Michigan, on a bill with country legends George Jones and Conway Twitty.

In November he played Sea World in San Antonio and told the crowd, "I love Texas. It's the only place that knows how to do Mexican food right—and chicken fried steak."

In December the roman decor at Caesar's Palace in Las Vegas went country when Vince opened for Reba McEntire for several nights in the Circus Maximus Showroom. It was the first time he'd played at a big venue in Vegas. The *Las Vegas Sun* sang his praises. It was a safe bet he'd be back.

> "I'm proud to be the neighborhood boy from Oklahoma. I care a lot about where I came from."
>
> —VINCE GILL

No crowd was more enthusiastic than the one assembled at the Woodward County Fair Building in Woodward, Oklahoma. Promoter K. C. Austin of Multi Talent Entertainment said only eight hundred fans were expected but there were about fifteen hundred packing the room, many standing around the perimeter. It was Vince Gill's first concert in his home state since winning the CMA Award.

Vince sang a lot of songs from *When I Call Your Name* and previewed some new ones. Folks just wanted to get near the stage and Vince convinced the security guards to let them come close. When the crowd asked for some bluegrass music, Vince obliged. He told his fellow Oklahomans that the night of the CMA Awards, "apart from the night my daughter was born, was the happiest night of my life."

Many of the young ladies at the concert were smitten with their hometown hero. They grabbed at his boots during one song, causing him to lose his place. After the show he said, "They were making me feel like Elvis."

The fourth hit from *When I Call Your Name* was "Never Knew Lonely." When it went to number three on the charts, the album went gold. It was now selling more than his previous four albums combined. It was also Tony Brown's first gold record for MCA.

"Never Knew Lonely" was a song Vince had written some years earlier when he was in Holland and had been separated from his family for an entire month. He missed his wife, Janis, and daughter, Jenifer, "so I decided to bring them this song instead of a teddy bear." He had recorded it while at RCA but it wasn't included on any of the three albums he released there. The song meant so much to him that he put it on his first album for MCA.

The vocals, including Vince doing backup with Billy Thomas and Harry Stinson, are beautifully layered. The guitar solo is an extension of the lyrics and the emotions they convey. As a man discovers the depth of loneliness when being separated from his loved ones, we all realize that until you've felt it, you can't understand it. This song makes us feel it. So does the video. Showing a man traveling on a road alone, it was shot in sepia tones that convey the mood. We see Vince alone in a room with his guitar and we're also treated to a nice close-up of his fingers playing the instrument. In one shot, he stands outside near a 1960s white Cadillac convertible, looking every bit as lonely as he sounds.

When "Never Knew Lonely" won a songwriter's award from the *Music City News* in 1991, Vince Gill wept during the televised show. He looked into the audience and realized he was seeing his daughter for the first time in a long time. "It stirred up a bunch of emotions," he said. "I know there are a lot of times she'd come home and I wouldn't be there."

The Grammy Awards, given to music in every field, are considered the highest honor of all in the business. Over eight thousand members of NARAS, the National Academy of Recording Arts and Sciences, cast their votes each year.

Vince Gill had made it to the top with one song. "When I Call Your Name" won a Grammy in February 1991 for Best Country Vocal Performance, Male.

Vince Gill's Grammy Awards

1990 Best Country Vocal Performance, Male,
for "When I Call Your Name"

1991 Best Country Vocal Collaboration
for the single "Restless" with Steve Wariner
and Ricky Skaggs, from the *Mark O'Connor
and the New Nashville Cats* album

1992 Best Country Song for "I Still Believe in You"

1992 Best Country Vocal Performance, Male,
for "I Still Believe in You"

1993 Best Country Instrumental
Performance for collaboration with
Asleep at the Wheel on "Red Wing"

1994 Best Country Vocal Performance, Male,
for "When Love Finds You"

1995 Best Country Vocal Performance, Male,
for "Go Rest High on That Mountain"

1995 Best Country Song for
"Go Rest High on That Mountain"

1996 Best Vocal Collaboration for
"High Lonesome Sound" with Alison
Krauss and Union Station

1996 Best Country Vocal Performance, Male,
for "Worlds Apart"

1997 Best Country Vocal Performance, Male,
for "Pretty Little Adriana"

CHAPTER SIX

Poet of the Heart

The Academy of Country Music Awards show in April 1991 presented a dilemma most husbands and wives would rather avoid. Vince Gill and Reba McEntire were nominated for best duet for "Oklahoma Swing" and Sweethearts of the Rodeo had a song up for the same award.

Fortunately, the Judds won.

"I don't think that's one I would like to have won," Vince said.

The first time Vince Gill was invited to sing at the Grand Ole Opry, he had to turn the venerable institution down. He had a previous engagement—his seven-year-old daughter Jenifer was in a talent show that Vince had agreed to play guitar for. The Opry folks understood and scheduled him for the following Saturday night.

Many people are invited to sing on the sacred stage of the Grand Ole Opry but few are chosen as members. In 1991, Vince Gill was inducted as the newest member of the Grand Ole Opry. This invitation to join country music's most exclusive club was not a result of his one big year but instead honored Vince for his long career in bluegrass and country.

Many people think the Ryman Auditorium in downtown Nashville was the Opry's first home, but in fact it was its sixth. "The Mother Church of Country Music," as the Ryman was affectionately called, housed the Grand Ole Opry from 1943 to 1974. By the time Vince was invited to join, the Grand Ole Opry was no longer in the Ryman Auditorium. In 1974, when Opryland opened several miles east of downtown, the Grand Ole Opry moved to a custom-built hall on the grounds of Opryland USA. At first, many of the veteran performers felt there was no history in their new quarters, but they soon realized that the show is the people, not the building. Still, in reverence to tradition, a piece of the Ryman stage was removed and carefully laid in the center of the new stage.

> "I have tremendous reverence for the years the Opry has been there and what it's accomplished for country music. I want to do my part to keep that legacy going."
>
> —VINCE GILL

Vince has always maintained a close relationship with the men and women who make up country music's older generation. He values his friendships with people like Porter Wagoner and Little Jimmy Dickens.

"It was a big deal for my family when I was a kid, to hear these people perform," Vince said. "I couldn't do what I'm able to do if they hadn't taught me. I want them to know I respect them and that I haven't forgotten about them."

Reba McEntire said the Opry had been a part of her life for as long as she could remember. When her parents took the kids to the movies, they'd wait for them in the car listening to the Grand Ole Opry. It was also the destination for a lot of McEntire family vacations. Such reverence on the part of performers is testament to the enduring power of the Opry. Garth Brooks has said that becoming a member would always be the highest honor he could receive in the music business.

"The first time I played and sang on the Opry, I'd never had a feeling like I had that night on stage," Vince said. "I know it sounds corny, but there was this warmth that went through me. I'd never had that happen before. It was an incredible feeling."

He told a reporter he loved the Opry because it honored the great people in country music even when they were no longer popular. "Our culture, once you're not in vogue anymore, cuts your legs off and says, 'See you later.' The Opry is not about that. If they're eighty years old and can't carry a tune, they're still out there singing. Nobody says, 'Sorry, you can't sing anymore. You're not popular.' "

Life on the road continued to be rewarding for Vince Gill and his band. He had assembled a stellar group that was a who's who of Nashville's best pickers: steel guitar and fiddle player John Huey, a master of both instruments; Tony King, a hugely respected guitarist; Jimmy Johnson, who had played with Roy Orbison, played bass for Vince; and Andrea Zonn, a fiddle wizard and harmony singer whom Vince had known from his bluegrass days.

The acclaim was rising. The crowds were getting larger and louder. Vince was happy. He said that winning the award "hasn't changed me a lick." But he also said, "I feel a little vindicated. I've been making records since 1983. . . . It's been a long, hard struggle. A lot of people gave up on me."

He had a good perspective on everything. "Everybody has their place and time when they shine," he said. "I was pretty comfortable with my success level before the award. I was working . . . having a great life. I wasn't down and out."

He wasn't going to make any apologies for his previous records. He wasn't blaming RCA for the difficulties he'd faced early in his country career. Nor would he say MCA was the only reason "When I Call Your Name" was played on the radio when other songs didn't get airplay. Instead he said, "We just managed to make a really good record that is selling like crazy." True. And his honey-sweet voice and inventive leads and elaborate guitar runs were finally reaching the fans who were giving Vince what he'd always dreamed of.

Tulsa City Limits is a great landmark, one of America's most exciting music clubs. Owner Gary Bentley and his lovely wife, Delaney, said the club was a rock and roll venue for its first year in business, then changed to country to fill the huge demand for some great country music. It has a huge dance floor, big video screens, and a sharp stage with bars all around. Tasty barbeque is available from Billy Ray's, a bbq joint right inside the club. Upstairs is a huge gallery where you can stand and watch the show below—and watch all those Tulsans scootin' their boots off in exciting displays of country line dancing.

Vince Gill is a favorite act at Tulsa City Limits. One measure of his enduring appeal there is that almost every night patrons do a dance they call the Southside Shuffle to "Turn Me Loose," Vince's first single from his RCA days.

Gary Delaney says the club's customers love Vince not

just because he's an Oklahoman. "You can't fool people in Tulsa," he said. "If you're good, they know it."

One of Vince Gill's Fender Telecaster guitars, complete with his autograph, graces the wall of Tulsa City Limits. Many other artists love to play there, too, among them hometown Tulsan Leon Russell, Little Texas, Toby Keith, Tracy Byrd, Clay Walker, Steve Wariner, and Mark Collie. Brooks & Dunn did their first show there and filmed some videos there, too. When various organizations hold contests for club of the year, many artists write in Tulsa City Limits as their favorite—even when it's not nominated!

More awards: In addition to giving Vince Gill a Top Ten Song of the Year Award for "When I Call Your Name," the TNN/Music City News Awards named Vince Gill the Instrumentalist of the Year in 1991. This was especially gratifying to Vince since at the time he was getting more attention for his voice than for his guitar playing. He made a comment that summed up his talents.

> "I try to play like a singer and sing like a player.
> Phrasing is what makes either great. It's where
> you put the notes, not how many."
>
> —VINCE GILL

People magazine interviewed Vince and Janis Gill in 1991. You know you've arrived when you keep showing up in the pages of one of the most popular magazines in the country. Janis told the reporter, "Vince hasn't changed at all since I first met him. He's still the same easygoing, aw-shucks sort of guy that he was the first day we met."

She went on to say that she and Vince were opposites in many ways. He listened to bluegrass while she enjoyed

Vince Gill's TNN/Music City News Awards

1990 Top Ten Song of the Year for
"When I Call Your Name"

1991 Instrumentalist of the Year

1991 Top Ten Song of the Year for
"Pocket Full of Gold"

1991 Top Ten Song of the Year for
"Never Knew Lonely"

1992 Top Ten Song of the Year for
"Look at Us"

1992 Song of the Year for
"I Still Believe in You"

1993 Top Ten Song of the Year for
"Don't Let Our Love Start Slippin' Away"

1993 Top Ten Song of the Year for
"One More Last Chance"

1994 Top Ten Song of the Year for
"Whenever You Come Around"

1994 Top Ten Song of the Year for
"Tryin' to Get Over You"

classical music. He played golf and she liked to sew. He was unorganized and she needed order. He was laid back and she was stressed out.

They also talked about the challenges of being a two-career couple. In their case, their jobs took them on the road a lot more than most people had to deal with. "Janis and I have been coming and going for so many years," Vince said, "that it's nothing new to anybody. We're both content in our relationship and content in what we're doing." They wanted to spend more time together, he said, but as artists pursuing success in the music business, they both knew from the start how it was going to be.

In late May 1991, the Myriad Convention Center in Oklahoma City was packed for a concert that gave financially strapped farmers a boost and gave fans a great show. Sixteen thousand fans to be exact, and they were cheering to the sounds of four giants from the state of Oklahoma. Garth Brooks, Joe Diffie, Restless Heart, and Vince Gill were putting their fame to work for the FARM (Farmers at Risk Matter) Fest.

The show lasted four and a half hours! Vince Gill's part of the show had the audience screaming, especially when he told the crowd the concert had sold more tickets than an Elvis Presley performance.

"We're bigger than Elvis tonight," he said. "That's been a dream of mine—to be bigger than Elvis."

Vince's guitar solos were described by one concertgoer as "simply spectacular," and he also showcased his voice on "Never Knew Lonely" and "When I Call Your Name."

At one point, he sent his band away for a break. He sang "Life in the Old Farm Town," a song he said he wrote based on the problems facing farm families whose way of life was threatened every day by debt, drought, and even suicide. "Remember why we came here," he told the crowd.

Vince continued writing songs in preparation for his second MCA album. "It's a lot easier for me to sing my own songs and try to get people to believe the things I feel," he said. "It's not that I'm a great poet, it's just better for me melodically." Vince was able to build songs around his own strengths and weaknesses as a singer.

He also said he'd rather sing with women than with men. "I'm a tenor and a lot of times it's hard to find guys who sing high enough," he said.

He tried out some of the new songs when he played a Houston club called Willie Nelson's Night Life. "Here's a song for everybody who's with somebody you shouldn't be," he said and the men laughed while the women cheered and whistled. Vince went on to amuse the crowd when he said, "I said the same thing at a Baptist school last week and nobody laughed." Then he sang a new song called "Pocket Full of Gold," a ballad some compared to the best of Gram Parsons.

The Houston crowd loved his concert version of "Oklahoma Swing," as Vince stretched the song out for more than ten minutes with his own guitar solos and the solos of fiddler Andrea Zonn and steel guitarist John Huey.

The bluegrass influence was prominent. "I've got a band now where I can put bluegrass on my shows again," Vince said and the crowd roared its approval. He was committed to keeping bluegrass alive, Vince said, even though it was unlikely it would ever hit the charts and have high sales figures. He wanted to have segments, in the right kind of shows, where he and his band could do twenty minutes of acoustic music. Even as he was finding

the success he'd always dreamed of, Vince Gill was still
devoted to his own vision as an artist. He was still doing it
all for the music.

It was the middle of 1991 and Vince was working on his
soon-to-be-released album *Pocket Full of Gold*. He was
spending time recording the album during the height of
the first album's success. For the first time in his many
years in the music business, he had an opportunity to work
in the studio secure in the knowledge that he was really
getting somewhere in his career. "It's a real feeling of ac-
complishment," he said. "It makes it a little easier to make
some decisions while you're recording."

When an artist makes it big for the first time, there's
enormous pressure to keep the momentum going. No
matter how long it took to create your first hit, you have to
get that second one out there pretty quickly to be remembered by fans who are bombarded all the time with new
artists and songs. A few more successful albums and you
will be considered an important artist for all time, but still,
your ability to continue year after year in music depends
on sustaining those levels of success. Perhaps that's one
of the reasons real artists long to be successful and to remain in the forefront of the fans' minds. When they reach
that point, they can have the luxury of taking their time to
craft the kind of songs and albums that reflect their artistic
vision.

"I hate to jinx it, but it's looking pretty good."
—VINCE GILL

Now it was clear that people loved Vince Gill as a
country artist. How rewarding to know that after fol-

"The nicest man in country music"

A glorious homecoming in 1993

Reba McEntire, Vince, Wynonna

A most generous golfer

With Jane Seymour and Merle Haggard

. . . Clint Black

. . . Patty Loveless

. . . Ricky Skaggs   . . . Trisha Yearwood

. . . Bonnie Raitt and Mary Chapin Carpenter

Gamma Liaison/Hilbun

Vince and Janis Gill

Globe/Redway

Vince sporting a goatee

Mom

Can't you just hear them now?

lowing your heart, as Vince had done when he'd committed himself to country music, tens of thousands of fans were confirming your choice by buying your record and coming to your concerts.

The second album was again produced by Tony Brown. Eight of its ten songs were written, or co-written, by Vince Gill. The title cut, "Pocket Full of Gold," written with Brian Allsmiller, tells the story of a man who puts his wedding ring in his pocket and sets into motion a pattern of deceit—cheating on his wife, lying to the woman he's cheating with, and helping himself to "another man's treasure" in the process. It's like a morality lesson gently told but plenty serious.

The vocal structure of the song is rich and complex, displaying the full range of Vince Gill's vocal power. It features background vocals by Vince and Patty Loveless in the same perfect blending of voices that had worked so well on "When I Call Your Name." Patty Loveless matches him and their voices blend together like sugar and cream. It's as if these two were born to sing together. Vince said he thinks Patty's voice "is one of the best we have in country music."

The "Pocket Full of Gold" video shows Vince performing the song from a stage in a roadside bar, playing a Gibson Jumbo acoustic guitar. He opens with the revealing lyric: "He slipped the ring off his finger." Couples are slow-dancing to the tune, holding one another tightly. The camera alternates between shots of the band onstage with Vince and scenes of a man being unfaithful and looking like he feels pretty awful about it. Singing much of the song with his eyes closed, wearing a great leather bomber jacket, Vince shows what a wonderful presence he is on the screen. The camera loves him—if he wanted a career in the movies, he'd be a screen idol, just as George Strait won the hearts of millions of women and the admiration of millions of men when he starred and sang in the movie *Pure Country*.

The album opens with "I Quit," written by Vince and Max D. Barnes. Herb Pedersen sings background vocals on a song about a guy who's had enough of falling in and out of love and says if he can't have the woman he's with, he's just going to quit at love. The sad message is counterpointed by the jaunty, almost western swing sound.

One of the most beautiful songs on the album—one of the most beautiful Vince Gill songs of all time, in some people's opinion—is "Look at Us," also written by Vince and Max D. Barnes. Background vocals are by Andrea Zonn, Vince's fiddle player, and Vince. The sweet sentiments about a couple still deeply in love after many years together were inspired, Vince said, by Janis. Vince said his wife inspires all his songs "in a roundabout way," but he never got so personal that no one else could relate to them. "She gets credit for the hits," he said sweetly, "but not the blame for the ones that don't make it. I just love her and I like to see her get some credit."

Another reason "Look at Us" is so special is that it really showcases Vince as a young artist who understands what traditional country is all about yet whose approach is fresh and new enough to bring that music into the next generation. He takes a classic theme of undying love and finds a new way to express it. Wouldn't it make a beautiful movie song?

The video for "Look at Us" is one of the loveliest ever made for a song. It is a collection of old photographs and home movies showing happy, loving couples, real people of all ages and backgrounds. They are smiling at each other and at the camera as the song is played, filled with its beautiful fiddle, piano, and steel guitar. Vince Gill the singer doesn't appear once. Images of Vince and Janis Gill are sprinkled throughout the images of the other loving couples. What a beautiful tribute to his wife and a great chance for fans to see the Gills together.

The song has become a Vince Gill classic. It is often played at weddings and at ceremonies when couples renew their vows. One man wanted the lyrics of "Look at Us" carved into his tombstone and, when his time came, his family obliged his request because he loved the song so much.

The next song is a change of pace. "The shuffle was the greatest groove country ever had," Vince said. "Ray Price hit home with it in the 1950s and I'd always wanted to write one."

That shuffle is "Take Your Memory," which Vince wrote by himself and which has background vocals by Herb Pedersen. It features the late great session drummer Larry London and Hargus "Pig" Robbins on piano. This song is another tip of the hat to old-time country music, the kind of sound that was heard on Saturday nights in the dance halls of Oklahoma where Vince's dad used to play. The subject matter is as old-time country as could be found on any album in the 1990s.

"The new album feels very relaxed and very comfortable to me."

—VINCE GILL

"*Pocket Full of Gold* hit a lot of different pockets musically," Vince said. "On this one I feel more at ease singing and recording songs that were a little more straight-ahead country."

"The Strings That Tie You Down" is another song of love coming to an end that is both sad and upbeat at the same time. The character of the song says that saying good-bye will really be final after cutting those strings, though it is hard to picture himself giving up his love. Written by Vince Gill, again with Max D. Barnes, it features a great fiddle solo by Andrea Zonn.

Vince wrote "Liza Jane" with Reed Nielsen. It's a real rocker with Billy Thomas on background vocals. The lead guitar solo played by Vince on the Fender Telecaster is exactly what that guitar was made for. The sound of the guitar is as unique as Vince's way of playing it.

The video for "Liza Jane" shows how adaptable Vince could be. At the beginning of the video, he is standing under an umbrella in the pouring rain telling viewers that he and his pals were planning to have lots of fun outdoors at the world-famous Broadway Drive-In in Dixon, Tennessee, about thirty miles outside of Nashville. They were gonna have fireworks and fabulous cars, beautiful guys and dolls and play on top of the concession stand, with lots of old movies on the screen. But the rain got in the way so they just took the party inside. Once the music starts, the party is so much fun it just goes to show that Vince can even make you forget about the rain.

Backed only by his own acoustic guitar playing, Vince sings the first verse of "If I Didn't Have You in My World" in an almost a cappella fashion, barely strumming the guitar to give himself a note to begin on. Then the other instruments join in, followed by a trademark "Pig" Robbins piano solo. Co-written with Jim Weatherly, the song once again manages to do what Vince does best, combine joy and sorrow in a tribute to both emotions.

"A Little Left Over," written by Vince, also features his great guitar playing, this time electric all the way. The song describes a workingman's dream—all the bills are paid, there's a honky tonk down the road, and he's got a little bit left over to spend on Saturday night.

T. J. Knight and Curtis Wright contributed "What's a Man to Do" to *Pocket Full of Gold*. They had to be proud of the way Vince tenderly and lovingly sang their story of a man who can't figure out what to do with a woman who has found someone new.

The album ends with the upbeat, Cajun-spiced "Sparkle," written by Jim Lauderdale, who's written a lot for George Strait, among others, and John Leventhal, known for his work with Shawn Colvin. It's a lot of fun to leap up and dance to.

In October 1991, Vince Gill co-hosted the annual CMA Awards with another terrific new country star, Clint Black. As usual, there were a number of big moments in that evening's program. But one of the biggest was when longtime country music fan President George Bush and his wife, Barbara, entered the Grand Ole Opry House and were seated with Crystal Gayle, Roy Acuff, and the Gatlin Brothers. The First Couple received a standing ovation. At the end of the show, they took the stage.

> "It's easy to see why America loves country music. Country music loves America."
> —PRESIDENT GEORGE BUSH

Vince won Male Vocalist of the Year. He also won for Vocal Event of the Year for his work as part of the New

Nashville Cats, a group consisting of himself, Mark O'Connor, Ricky Skaggs, and Steve Wariner. Vince and Tim DuBois also shared the Song of the Year award, which is given to the songwriter, for "When I Call Your Name." Vince was thrilled. He felt this award was even more significant than the Male Vocalist Award. "This was the most important to me because there are a lot of people who didn't think I was a great songwriter and still may not." He laughed. "They just think I got lucky."

By November, *Pocket Full of Gold* was racing up the charts. It was also pushing the sales of *When I Call Your Name* even higher. And with the second album and his first Male Vocalist of the Year CMA Award, Vince's road schedule got even busier. As he acknowledged, success meant he had to work even harder and spend even more time on the road. The reality of the music business is that you can't get hits without touring to build an audience, and you can't build an audience without the hits. But he was happy. "Now the music's speaking for itself," he said. "It's a great feeling."

Just before Christmas 1991, viewers tuned in to watch "The Tonight Show Starring Johnny Carson." Johnny's first two guests that night were actor Burt Reynolds, who charmed everyone as he always does, and a very funny comedian named Al Lubell, who had the audience cheering. When it came time for Johnny to introduce his musical guest, he held up a copy of the new CD, *Pocket Full of Gold*, and introduced Vince Gill. Johnny told the audience that the horn section from Doc Severinsen's Tonight Show Orchestra would be joining Vince in his first song. Then the audience at home and in the studio were treated to a superb performance of "Oklahoma Swing," made even better by a long guitar solo. The song sounded great and Vince Gill, the artist and musician, looked completely at home jamming and playing with Doc's great players.

Dressed in a white shirt, tuxedo jacket, blue jeans, and shining boots, Vince then sang "Look at Us," playing a jet black guitar with a cow-patterned strap. His voice and guitar-playing had the audience mesmerized. What's interesting now, looking back at that performance, is how much time Vince was given for his first appearance on the king of all national entertainment and talk shows. Today, artists are often asked to play shortened versions of their hits when they appear as musical guests on these shows. But in 1991, Vince Gill was not only given the chance to play two songs (that hardly ever happens anymore), but he was able to play those songs fully and richly, even including long guitar solos.

When he was done, he got the endorsement of Johnny Carson that all guests yearn for but not all receive. Smiling from ear to ear, Johnny Carson called out, "Yeah, Vince!" Ask any comedian or musician who's been on the "Tonight Show" what it means to get the thumbs-up from Johnny, or his successor Jay Leno, and you'll know how great this was for Vince.

Another major reward on the "Tonight Show" is being asked to come sit with the other guests after your performance. Johnny waved Vince over and said, "Good to see you, Vince. Thanks for being with us."

Vince shook hands with Burt Reynolds and with Johnny's number-one pal Ed McMahon and took a seat right next to Johnny. "Vince will be doing the 'Music of Christmas' on NBC on December 15," Johnny said. "Not to be confused with Burt and Loni doing the Super Bowl on New Year's Day." Vince just cracked up laughing, as did Burt and Ed.

President George Bush and First Lady Barbara Bush were joined by many of the nation's lawmakers and other top government officials and dignitaries in the historic National Building Museum in the nation's capital for what had become a decade-long tradition. "Christmas in Washington" was a special musical celebration of the Yuletide season for the benefit of the Children's Hospital National Medical Center of Washington, D.C.

The Eastern High School Choir of Washington, D.C., the U.S. Naval Academy Glee Club, and the U.S. Army Herald Trumpets entertained the assembled guests with all the professionalism and excellent music people had come to expect from these distinguished groups.

Then four of the most beautiful voices in contemporary American music filled the hall with a variety of traditional carols, gospel songs, and contemporary seasonal music. Those voices belonged to Anne Murray, Johnny Mathis, Anita Baker, and Vince Gill. Close your eyes and just imagine what a wonderful evening it was.

In May 1992, Vince did something most new artists shy away from: He played Branson, Missouri.

Branson has wonderful activities for families and kids, plenty of good golfing, and three beautiful lakes—Table Rock Lake, Bull Shoals Lake, and Lake Taneycomo—that make up what is known as the trilakes area. Every imaginable water sport is available, or one can just ride the showboat *Branson Belle*. But the real reason millions flock to Branson each year is for the music. Many of the giants who paved the way for the big success being enjoyed by country music today—folks like Mel Tillis, Charley Pride, Box Car Willie, Roy Clark, and Mickey Gilley—have theaters in Branson bearing their names. So do other music stars, like Andy Williams, Bobby Vinton, and Tony Orlando. Shows go on all day and night, and the theaters also contain stores where fans can purchase souvenirs and star memorabilia.

Vince wasn't sure his current radio hits would play as well on stage in Branson as the songs of the more established classic artists, who had been making hits when he was still a young boy just learning to play. But he wanted to pay homage to them. "A lot of those people are the ones I learned how to play music from, so I have a great deal of respect for them," he said.

> "I've had guys come up to me and say, 'Man, we'd like to do "When I Call Your Name," but nobody in the band can sing high enough.' "
> —VINCE GILL

In his typically generous way, Vince acknowledged his place in the country music hit parade. "Even as popular as I am now," he said, "it still doesn't translate into what Conway Twitty or Merle Haggard have done over the last thirty years."

By the time he played there for the first time, Vince's song "Liza Jane" was one of the songs most often performed by Branson artists. Each one did the song a little differently. But to Vince that didn't matter. "No matter how well or how poorly someone chooses to play something you've written or recorded, that's not the exercise," he said. "It's that someone thought enough of it to do it."

"I know there're a lot of sound-alikes out there, and that's something I don't want to be," Vince said. "I'm not consciously singing a different way. I just open my mouth and sing like I hear or feel it."

Vince Gill was carving out a very distinctive place for himself in the world of country music. In the early 1990s, country music was growing in all directions, fueled in part by the phenomenal success of Garth Brooks. The experts who were helping to market Garth's amazing new rockin' country sound were pointing out every chance they got that, because of Garth, millions of new record buyers were turning on to country music every month. Country radio stations were also getting more pumped up than ever before by the new listeners who found something exciting in Garth and were now tuning in to see what else they'd like to check out in country music.

So many of these new listeners were those frustrated by what they found when they turned on their old favorite rock and pop radio stations. They weren't finding the good old rock and roll songs with a great beat, the songs they'd danced to and had fun with growing up. They weren't finding the engaging lyrics, interesting musical direction, and hopeful message of the singer/songwriters they had grown to love in the sixties and seventies. Instead, listeners to rock and pop stations were finding grunge, rap, hip-hop, and songs about subjects that were not only alien to their lives but often filled with violence.

These were the baby boomers—Vince Gill's contemporaries—who hadn't listened to much music during the 1980s when their priorities were career, family, and mortgages. Now, in the nineties, they had some breathing room. They returned to record stores and radio only to find that the music and its message, for the first time in their lives, did not reflect their views and experiences. Much of it was about despair in a world without hope. Here was an audience doing better financially than their parents, who had young families, nice homes, and everything to hope for. All their lives they had turned to radio to hear about their own lives from the folks they admired. Now they found people whining, playing harsh music, and declaring the end of the world as we know it. Melody and harmony were nowhere to be found. Even the sensuality of r&b had been changed into rap and hip hop that mainly relied on samples, where people take an electronic snippet of another song to provide the rhythmic background for lyrics that, quite often, either said very little or something very raw.

Where was the generation for whom music was so important going to turn for the kind of music that reflected their real lives? Well, they kept pushing the buttons on the radio and found not only Garth Brooks but a whole gang of new musicians to listen to. Vince Gill and George Strait and Alan Jackson and all the other country stars at the top or rising in the early 1990s were playing music that may not have been about the suburbs and the shopping malls but was at least about life and love and real people. Their songs were stories, with characters going through heartfelt moments that the baby boomers could relate to. Add the fact that a lot of the music had a good beat and you could dance to it, and suddenly country was hip.

Vince Gill's decision to recommit himself to country music coincided with, and probably contributed to, the rising sales of country music all over America. So did that other new element in American life—the computer. As the 1990s began, a new technology called SoundScan was introduced into retail establishments. Now those handy bar codes were used to count record sales the same way sales of grocery products were counted, and those figures became the source of the *Billboard* magazine and other critical industry charts. The facts were clear: Country albums were selling all over the place. Longtime country fans had known all along that their music wasn't just some poor cousin of rock and roll, but it took computers to make the rest of the world aware of this fact.

This revelation prompted CNN to do a story reporting that in cities and suburbs across America—areas that weren't traditionally regarded as country music markets— country was rising and rock music falling in popularity. Vince Gill was asked for his comments: "I don't really see the demise of rock and roll. I just think that lyrically and musically, country's a great form of music for people to get into."

In 1992, the Nashville Network offered its viewers a very special show, "A Celebration of Eddy Arnold." There was plenty to celebrate. Arnold, who'd grown up on a farm and attended a one-room schoolhouse in Tennessee, was playing guitar by the age of ten and playing at square dances soon after to help support his family following his father's death. He went on to become one of the most beloved entertainers in pop and country singing. He spent more weeks at number one than any other artist, with such songs as "Bouquet of Roses" in the 1940s, "I'd Trade All My Tomorrows (for Just One Yesterday)" in the 1950s, and "Make the World Go Away" in the 1960s, just to name a few. In 1966, he was elected to the Country Music Hall of Fame, and in 1967, he was named CMA's Entertainer of the Year. Most of today's country stars say they grew up listening to Eddy Arnold. Even one of the youngest stars, LeAnn Rimes, paid tribute to Arnold by singing "Cattle

Call" with him on her first major label album, the phenomenal *Blue*.

Vince performed on the show with Arnold and with another big star the Gills all loved, Chet Atkins. It was a huge honor to be asked to share the stage with such legends of country music.

"My dad has every Eddy Arnold record and Chet Atkins record ever made," Vince said. "So for me to be playing with them made me realize, through his eyes, how far I'd come."

CHAPTER SEVEN

Taking It to the Top

The Lloyd Noble Center, on the campus of the University of Oklahoma, is the place where circuses, ice skating shows, basketball games of the Oklahoma Sooners, and numerous other events take place. Here, in Norman, on a Friday night in March 1992, more than 7,300 country music fans were getting the treat of their lives. Three of the biggest country stars around were fixing to entertain the fine citizens of greater Oklahoma City.

George Jones opened the show. He sang many of his greatest hits including "The Race Is On," "He Stopped Loving Her Today," "Tennesee Whiskey," and "I'm a One-Woman Man." Conway Twitty closed the show with a medley of some of his numerous hits—"Hello Darlin'," "Tight Fitting Jeans," "Crazy in Love," "The Rose," and "That's My Job." And right in between these two towering legends was a relatively new voice in country, one of the city's most important contributions to the world of great music, Norman's very own Vince Gill.

Vince opened his set with "Victim of Life's Circumstances" and "Cinderella" and continued with his more recent hit songs. In "Oklahoma Swing," he showcased the talents of his band by giving each member a long solo. He finished the show with "When I Call Your Name," but the crowd wooed him back for an encore of "Oklahoma Borderline."

When the time came for Vince's third MCA album, he took some time off from touring to write some new songs. *When I Call Your Name* was already considered a country classic. He had proven with *Pocket Full of Gold* that he didn't have the so-called sophomore jinx, a fear of many recording artists and their record companies that an artist may be capable of only one big success. Vince Gill had the record sales, the concert attendance, and the industry awards. Now he was comfortable as a star, ready to relax and work on the music.

One reason Vince felt more at ease in preparing for the new album was that he had learned so much from the last two. "*When I Call Your Name* was very diverse," he said. "We tried a little bit of everything. On *Pocket Full of Gold* we narrowed it down, maybe too much. With this album, we'll try to get the best of both."

"Emotion is the truest form of life. To me, it's the most important one, really."
—VINCE GILL

He talked about his songwriting for the upcoming album, saying he wanted the songs to touch on as many emotions as possible. He was trying to be emotional without being too personal. "People don't want to hear just about me when I write songs," he said. "They want to have lyrics that pertain to how they feel and what goes on in their lives."

Vince Gill's songwriting had always been good, but now he was growing into the ranks of exceptional creators of the best kinds of songs—beautiful stories presented through just the right kind of music that itself helps convey the meaning of the tales. Anyone who thinks it's easy to write a song needs only to try to do it. We've all heard, loved, and sung along with hundreds of songs that seem so simple and direct that the craft of songwriting looks easy. But it's just that simplicity and directness that take the ultimate in talent, patience, and perseverance.

Think of the lyrics in "When I Call Your Name." In just a few verses, the story of a life is revealed. Some songs will stuff a million details in to try to paint a picture, but with just a few brush strokes, Vince and Tim DuBois give us a note on a table in a once happy but now silent home and we are left to bring our own emotional understanding to the story. The three simple words in the song and the title "Look at Us" speak volumes about a man's pride in the love he has shared with a woman for many years. When songwriters can convey so much story and sub- stance in so few words, they leave space for the listener to become part of the story.

"I like simplicity," Vince said. "I wear my heart on my sleeve and my own emotions just kind of come out, good or bad." He said he'd had a lot of people tell him his songs say what they wish they could say. "That's a neat feeling, to have someone like your lyrics to make them think they feel the same things you do."

Most of the time in Nashville, the songwriters are not the ones who actually sing the songs. Very few of the major recording and performing artists in country music actually write their own songs. While singer/songwriters from other musical genres have been coming to Nashville in recent years, the long tradition in Music City is of two separate camps, the songwriters and the singers. Vince

Gill was an exception to this. Being a singer himself brought a whole new dimension to his songwriting. It's one thing to write a song without having any idea who might eventually sing it. It's quite another to write a song tailored to your own voice and style, to your own special phrasings, and to hear yourself singing it while you're writing it.

You also already know it's going to be on an album, making you the envy of all the songwriters who toil away, crafting beautiful songs that might never make the cut.

Vince Gill spent a lot of time writing the songs for the third album, so much time that one day he realized he was sacrificing valuable golf time to write them. "That's scary," he said. But it was worth it.

The aspect of his personality that was continuing to show itself in his songs was the one that had already touched the hearts of his fans.

> "I love the romantic part of life and I love that part of a song, so ninety-nine percent of my songs are about love and relationships."
>
> —VINCE GILL

It was his observation that throughout their lives people think about love and romance more than anything else. "I know it's what I remember in a song," he said.

One reason for Vince's appeal to men and women of all ages is that the themes of his love songs are timeless. They aren't about sex. They're about love.

"It's ten times more gratifying to love someone and have them love you than it is to have sex with them," he said. "I mean, don't get me wrong—that's a nice thing, too! Real love . . . has a much deeper feeling, it's a much richer feeling, it has more substance."

That strong emotion is deeply apparent in the title of the third big Vince Gill album from MCA. *I Still Believe in You* was released in 1992, once again produced by Tony Brown.

The album explores many emotional situations, beginning with the soulful plea of the first cut, "Don't Let Our Love Start Slippin' Away," written by Vince and keyboard player Pete Wasner. There's great interplay between the acoustic and electric guitars, layered as only Vince can, and Pete Wasner's keyboard is extremely tasteful. While the lyrics are the focus here of a rather serious subject— the threat of losing a good love—the underlying rhythms make you tap your toe. The song shows you can rock while still being true to country. It was the second single from the album and an instant hit.

"No Future in the Past," written by Vince and Carl Jackson, has a high, wailing chorus. It's a waltz and the chorus really makes you feel the emotional urgency of the lyric. "Nothing Like a Woman," written by Vince and Reed Nielsen, seems to show that all really soulful music comes from the same place—the heart. Vince demonstrates that he has as much soul in his tenor voice as such great Motown singers as Smokey Robinson of Smokey Robinson and the Miracles or David Ruffin of the Temptations. The song could just as easily have come out of Detroit in the 1960s as Nashville in the 1990s. It shows that Vince had absorbed the influence of all the best music he grew up listening to.

Vince is the sole writer on "Tryin' to Get Over You." Building slowly to the chorus, the song is about a loneliness that will never go away for the singer: As he says, it will take dying to get over his love. The plaintive vocal treatment of the story would get that message across even if you didn't understand the language being spoken.

"Say Hello," written by Vince and Pete Wasner, is a smooth dance tune for dancing close on a Saturday night. It's a real traditional country lyrical subject. The casual message of "Say Hello" is delivered like a walking bass part that evokes memories of Bakersfield country music in the sixties.

But sweetness and romance isn't all Vince Gill can do—not by a long shot. Just listen to "One More Last Chance," written with Gary Nicholson. Here's a song about a fellow who just likes to party and make noise with his "good ol' boys" down at the honky tonk but whose wife does not take kindly to his spending more time with them than with her. When she greets him at the door holding a Bible and a rolling pin, he does his best to assure her he's not running around, just out having fun with the guys. Listeners are the ones really having fun—with Vince's guitar solo and the harmonica and fiddle.

In the lyrics of "One More Last Chance," the woman decides to take away the guy's car keys so he can't drive back to the honky tonk, but as the lyrics say, "she forgot about my old John Deere." Perhaps Vince is making a teasing reference to the story about the day George Jones took his lawn tractor into town when he couldn't drive his car. The song embodies all the best of Vince, a sense of humor and exceptional ability to play, sing, and create a song that's a lot of fun—what music is all about.

The video for "One More Last Chance" is just as much fun as the song. Its sets are two of Vince's favorite courses, the Nashville Golf and Athletic Club and the Golf Club of Tennessee. As the music entertains our ears, we feast our eyes on one of the wackiest games of golf ever played, alternating with a casual performance by Vince in the clubhouse. Some of Vince's real-life golfing buddies appear in the video, but by far the most surprising guest is George Jones riding his John Deere lawn mower.

"Under These Conditions," written by Vince and Max D. Barnes, is a song for those who look for answers to the dilemmas in their own lives. It's a song of conscience about a man and a woman who want each other but, even more, want to do the right thing by their own spouses and families.

"Pretty Words" was written by Vince and legendary songwriter Don Schlitz, who scored his first big number one when Kenny Rogers recorded his song "The Gambler" in 1978. He went on to have a string of hits with songs for the Nitty Gritty Dirt Band and Randy Travis as well as Garth Brooks and Mary Chapin Carpenter. He even wrote "Midnight Girl/Sunset Town" for the Sweethearts of the Rodeo. "Pretty Words" gets a bluegrass treatment. It's a warning that pretty words are just that, and they can get a girl in trouble. "Love Never Broke Anyone's Heart," written by Vince and Jim Weatherly, is a philosophical statement: It's not love that breaks your heart, it's what you do with love that hurts.

The title song and the second hit single from *I Still Believe in You* was inspired by Vince's wife, Janis, as he has said is the case for many of his songs. But this time it was the result of an argument they'd had. With such a busy and demanding schedule now that he was becoming a bigger and bigger star, Vince made an appointment to write music with piano player John Jarvis on a day he had originally planned to spend with his family. Janis was upset and they argued before he left. Whatever else Vince and

Jarvis may have planned to write that day, one result of their collaboration is the now-classic "I Still Believe in You." Rarely has a man apologized to a woman with such sincerity and obvious sadness for the pain he realizes he has caused. There isn't a woman on earth who wouldn't be touched by the beauty of the emotion conveyed in the song. Janis Gill said she cried when she heard it. Who wouldn't?

The sentiment in the lyric is given the spotlight here with the music acting as its foundation. It is as self-revealing as an artist can get—sharing not only his emotions but his life. He admits he's not perfect—a modern sentiment for men in country music.

One reviewer said the song "starts to rise from the speakers like vapors from a freshly baked cherry pie" and gave "I Still Believe in You" the ultimate accolade, calling it "the best country song to come out this year." Some people disagree—they call it one of the best songs ever written in any genre. It spent two weeks at number one on the country music charts. If radio programmers weren't so locked in to categories, it's a song that would have hit the top of the pop charts, too. It's the kind of song that touches the heart of everyone who hears it, proving that great lyrics and beautiful music don't know any categories.

I Still Believe in You is a much smoother album than the last two in the songs, the lyrical phrasing. With each new release, Vince showed an incredible growth and confidence in himself as an artist, writer, musician, and performer. That growth is what sets a real artist apart from a flash in the pan who only tries to re-create his first success by painting the same picture time after time.

Now, how many country music songs manage to make it into the hallowed pages of *Forbes* magazine? Well, it just so happens that Vince Gill's "One More Last Chance" was one of two songs in 1992 that made reference to John Deere lawn tractors. (The other was Joe Diffie's Top 10 hit "John Deere Greene.") According to *Forbes*, many of Deere's 2,500 independent dealers heard the two songs and jumped on the bandwagon, setting up promotional tie-ins with their local country radio stations. How many more sales of John Deere tractors resulted from this is not entirely clear, but as a John Deere spokesman said, "We don't do anything to solicit these songs, but we enjoy the heck out of 'em."

Even with the success of the more rockin' songs like "Liza Jane" and "One More Last Chance," Vince was still mainly known as a balladeer. He had no objections to this, believing that about 80 percent of the songs that become classics or standards were ballads. "I know what I'm like as a listener and I don't want to hear how happy you are. I like the blues," he said. "Songs like 'He Stopped Loving Her Today' and 'Crazy,' they kill you and people take them to heart."

I Still Believe in You enjoyed great reviews, spawned a number of hit singles, and placed Vince Gill firmly at the top of country's pantheon of stars. After all the lean years slowly climbing the ladder of success, it was clear that Vince Gill was really in it for the music. If money or major stardom were all he was after, he might not have tried for as long as he did.

He was still the same old Vince, still mainly interested in playing and singing. And in some ways he was thankful that the success didn't happen right away. "That's real dangerous, to go to the top and be the rage," he said. "It doesn't allow time to build. The way down might be just as quick."

Vince Gill had always unselfishly shared his talent, and therefore had always been able to do many different things with his music. He was still just as eager as he'd always been to contribute his talents to other people's records, even though some advised him that this constant participation might overexpose him.

"I think those things that I contribute to other people's records are as important as what they're contributing to the record. When I'm singing on one of Patty's [Loveless] records and it comes on the radio, I turn it up and I'm as excited about that as I am hearing my own."

> "Everything has changed, except my perception of what I'm doing and how I feel about it."
> —VINCE GILL

For the CMA Awards show in 1992, Vince Gill and Reba McEntire were asked to be the hosts. Once again, Oklahomans were center stage, showing off all their character and common sense in front of a huge national audience on the one night a year when everyone in America went country. One of those Oklahomans also showed off his famous sense of humor. Vince said that his main goal for the evening was to be a good host and "to change clothes more times than Reba," referring to the famous redhead's by-now legendary concerts, with their amazing stage productions and wardrobe surprises. Vince went on to say that he wasn't sure he could accomplish his goal, "but I've got two hours." He was right, he couldn't. Reba changed her clothes five times that evening.

"Look at Us" won Song of the Year and, for the second year in a row, Vince Gill was the CMA Male Vocalist of the Year.

* * *

In November 1992, MCA Records executives Bruce Hinton and Tony Brown surprised Vince with a platinum album plaque for *I Still Believe in You*. It was his third platinum album for the label and the fastest-selling one to date.

The celebration of Vince Gill's superstar status continued at the Bluebird Cafe at the end of January 1993. It was a "Number One Party," one of the most exciting parties to have in a town that throws its share of fun-filled events. The party was given by BMI, Broadcast Music, Inc., one of the agencies that collects income for songwriters and publishers. The other main agency is ASCAP, the American Society of Composers, Authors, and Publishers.

It's rare to have three number ones to celebrate at one party, but BMI had three Vince Gill hits to crow about. "I Still Believe in You" and "Take Your Memory with You," both written solely by Vince Gill, and "Don't Let Our Love Start Slippin' Away," written by Vince and Pete Wasner.

March 1993 brought some very sad news to Vince Gill and his family. His older brother, Bob, died of a heart attack. It was a sad ending to a life that had been troubled for many years. A car wreck earlier in his life had left Bob in a coma for several months. Afterward, he led a rough life, rambling around the country, sometimes disappearing for months at a time. Fortunately, he made it home to Oklahoma City right before his death.

Vince said of his brother, "He got dealt what he got dealt, but he never complained. And he showed me more character with nothing than most people who have everything."

Vince Gill's BMI Awards

1987 Most Performed Songs for "Oklahoma Borderline" and "If It Weren't for Him"

1991 Most Performed Songs for "When I Call Your Name," "Oklahoma Swing," and "Never Knew Lonely"

1992 Songwriter of the Year

1992 Most Performed Songs for "I Still Believe in You," "Look at Us," "Pocket Full of Gold," "Liza Jane," and "Here We Are"

1993 Most Performed Songs for "I Still Believe in You," "Don't Let Our Love Start Slippin' Away," and "Take Your Memory with You"

1995 Songwriter of the Year

1996 Most Performed Songs for "Which Bridge to Cross, Which Bridge to Burn" and "You Better Think Twice"

1997 Most Performed Songs for "Go Rest High on That Mountain" and "Pretty Little Adriana"

Oklahoma was well represented in the 1993 Country Music Association Awards nominations when they were announced in August. Several native Oklahomans, proud citizens of the Sooner State, were up for major awards.

Garth Brooks was nominated for four, including what would be his third straight Entertainer of the Year award. Tulsa's Ronnie Dunn, along with his partner Kix Brooks, received two nominations when Brooks & Dunn were included in the categories Vocal Duo of the Year and Entertainer of the Year.

> "Four Sooners Vie for Top Awards in Country Music."
>
> —*Daily Oklahoman*

But it was Oklahoma's own Vince Gill who walked away with the most—a total of eight nominations, the most since Merle Haggard's nine in 1970. The nominations were: Single of the Year and Best Music Video—"Don't Let Our Love Start Slippin' Away"; Album of the Year—*I Still Believe in You,* with its title song nominated for Song of the Year; two nominations for Vocal Event of the Year—one with Reba McEntire on the duet Vince performed with her, "The Heart Won't Lie," and one for his work with many other artists on George Jones's "I Don't Need Your Rockin' Chair"; and last but not least, the two big ones: Male Vocalist of the Year and Entertainer of the Year.

"What an honor to follow in the footsteps of Merle Haggard," Vince said. "I can't believe it."

It wasn't only the members of the CMA who believed in Vince Gill. The producers of the annual CMA Awards show, televised nationally, also believed he was the right man to host the show—this time all by himself. His warmth and obvious love for the task, along with the love and support of everyone in the audience, made Vince Gill a great choice to host one of the best parties country music has all year.

Vince said he was ready to take over the podium by himself, after having co-hosted the awards with Clint Black in l991 and with Reba McEntire in 1992. "It's fun and I'm pretty flattered that they entrust me with it," he said. "I never think hard about it being on television. I really just feel like I'm playing to the folks in the house."

Even for his first time hosting alone, Vince was comfortable. His easy manner no doubt helped everyone else feel a bit less nervous about performing and presenting awards before a live television audience that grew each year the CMA Awards were broadcast. His wit was as sharp as ever. After making a joke about the postmaster general of the United States, Vince's eyes twinkled as he said, "I probably shouldn't have said that. Two years ago, I slammed President Bush and got audited."

Vince said one part of the fun for him was the pressure of the clock. "It's kind of interesting when you're two minutes long or you need to make it thirty seconds longer," he said. "The evening lasts for three hours and you can get pretty out there in time if a winner decides to thank the whole world." He said his goal was to have fun and try to stay comfortable. It helped that he wasn't afraid to make fun of himself if he made a mistake.

Hosting was fun but even more fun was Vince's third win as Male Vocalist of the Year, his awards for Album of the Year and Song of the Year for "I Still Believe in You," and his inclusion in the Vocal Event of the Year award with many of his fellow musicians for the George Jones song "I Don't Need Your Rockin' Chair."

But the biggest moment of the evening was still to come. Traditionally, the last award of the evening is Entertainer of the Year, the big one. The members of the Country Music Association are asked to cast their vote for the one act whose records, concerts, and overall performance have been the best—and that's not easy in a business where there are always so many excellent achievements by the many artists who make country so great.

Nominated for Entertainer of the Year in 1993 were the amazing duo Brooks & Dunn, the one and only Garth Brooks, country great Alan Jackson, and one of the best women of country ever, Reba McEntire. Oh, yes, Vince Gill was also nominated. As the *Daily Oklahoman* had noted, of the six nominees in this category, four of them were from the Sooner State!

When the winner was announced, everyone gathered in the Grand Ole Opry House exploded in applause. The 1993 CMA Entertainer of the Year was their good friend, Vince Gill.

"I've always operated under the theory that I don't feel like I'm an entertainer," Vince said graciously and modestly about his win. "I just feel like I'm a musician and I sing songs."

The next week, an editorial ran in the *Daily Oklahoman* entitled "We Still Believe in Gill." Vince was continuing Oklahoma's leadership of country music, the newspaper noted, and said, "The easygoing singer is a class act." The paper offered its congratulations to Vince Gill for "the astonishing five trophies he garnered."

The scene at the Will Rogers Airport in Oklahoma City was one of excitement and anticipation on a Wednesday afternoon later in October. Country music fans were singing and clapping. Local dignitaries, including the mayor of Oklahoma City, Ron Norick, were tapping their feet to the music from the radio stations that had started setting up their equipment at around eleven that morning. Many people had arrived way before eleven, heeding the advice of Rick Buchanan of Oklahoma Events to avoid the expected traffic congestion. Traffic was heavy—with special parking set up in a grassy field east of Airport Terminal Drive to accommodate the expected crowds.

Everyone in the crowd was proud to be part of the big event but no one was prouder than Vince's mom, Jerene Gill, and Gena and Richard LeBeouf, his sister and brother-in-law. They were there to help welcome their dear son and brother, the one and only Vince Gill, back home to Oklahoma City after he had just become the CMA's Entertainer of the Year.

The plane arrived from Nashville. As usual, it took Vince a while to get through the airport—lots of people stopped and asked for autographs and he happily signed his name for them.

As the hundreds of fans waited, the singers from the Northwest Classen Cryslurs, a choral group from Vince's alma mater, prepared to sing for the man with the best voice in America.

When Vince Gill came out of the terminal, the crowd went crazy, welcoming their hometown hero with all the pride and love that is part of the spirit of Oklahoma. A few people were crying with joy.

But that was nothing compared to the moment Mayor Norick unveiled a large sign that all travelers would see

Vince Gill's Country Music Association Awards

1990 Single of the Year for "When I Call Your Name"

1991 Male Vocalist of the Year

1991 Song of the Year for "When I Call Your Name"

1991 Vocal Event of the Year along with Steve Wariner, Ricky Skaggs, and Mark O'Conner for *Mark O'Connor and the New Nashville Cats*

1992 Male Vocalist of the Year

1992 Song of the Year for "Look at Us"

1993 Entertainer of the Year

1993 Album of the Year for *I Still Believe in You*

---

upon leaving the airport. It said, "Welcome to Oklahoma City, Home of Vince Gill." Vince was beaming when the mayor shook his hand and gave him a proclamation and resolution from the city council proclaiming "Vince Gill Week."

It had been eighteen years since a young Vince Gill, armed only with his guitar and his talent, had left Oklahoma City with a dream in his heart but no way of knowing if he could make it as a musician. Now, having won the highest honor in country music, he was basking in the love of his fellow citizens.

1993 Song of the Year for
"I Still Believe in You"

1993 Male Vocalist of the Year

1993 Vocal Event of the Year (with other
artists) for "I Don't Need Your
Rockin' Chair" with George Jones

1994 Entertainer of the Year

1994 Male Vocalist of the Year

1994 Album of the Year (with other artists) for
Common Threads: Songs of the Eagles

1995 Male Vocalist of the Year

1996 Vocal Event of the Year for "I Will
Always Love You" with Dolly Parton

1996 Song of the Year for "Go Rest
High on That Mountain"

The Northwest Classen Cryslurs did their best to entertain the Entertainer of the Year. Then three members of the
choir, a young man and two young women, presented
Vince with a T-shirt and made him an honorary member of
the choir.

After Vince shook the young man's hand and kissed the
cheeks of the two young women, one of them declared she
would never wash her cheek again.

The mother of four young girls who had wanted to skip
school to go to the celebration had told her daughters they
couldn't do that. Instead, she would come to the airport

and get Vince's autograph. He obliged, and she was able to bring home four autographed fans that read, "I'm a Vince Gill Fan."

As a plane flew overhead with a streaming banner that said "Oklahoma City Loves Vince Gill," Ken Townsend, chairman of the Oklahoma City Chamber of Commerce, presented Vince with one of the many gifts he received from city officials, local businesses, and fans. Radio station representatives were thrilled to present gifts to a star who'd had so many hits and had given their listeners so many hours of great music. Byron Price, the executive director of the National Cowboy Hall of Fame and Western Heritage Center, presented Vince with a sculpture.

The moment finally came when Vince was ready to address the crowd. Looking at the shining, happy faces of the folks who loved him best, he told them that Oklahoma had given him two of its greatest assets and how much those assets had helped him in his career.

> "This is a state where character is very apparent. It's character I have in my heart. I want to do nice things for people."
>
> —VINCE GILL

The other asset he talked about was common sense. He told his friends and neighbors that common sense takes care of a lot of "you know, it's what's sitting out there in the pastures."

In the truly genuine generous spirit that is Vince Gill, he thanked the Oklahoma City schools for giving him a good education, mentioning the names of some of his former schoolteachers and music teachers. And, of course, he thanked his mother.

Jerene Gill's eyes were twinkling and she was smiling when Mayor Norick presented her with a street sign that said "Vince Gill Avenue." He told her that someday an Oklahoma City street would be named after her son.

When the event was over and police were attempting to escort Vince to a waiting car, he continued to sign autographs and greet some of the people who loved his home state as much as he does. "Oklahoma people are truly the salt of the earth," he said, and everyone agreed.

The next day, Vince hosted the Vince Gill Festival of the Horse Celebrity Golf Tournament.

Many recording artists make Christmas albums. Record companies love them because they sell year after year. Artists who love to sing can't help but enjoy stretching their pipes on the wonderful classic Christmas carols everyone can sing along with. Vince Gill's perfectly pitched voice, as comfortable and inviting as an old friend, seems made for Christmas.

He released his first Christmas album in the fall of 1993. Entitled *Let There Be Peace on Earth*, it featured such classics as "Do You Hear What I Hear," "Have Yourself a Merry Little Christmas," "What Child Is This," and "I'll Be Home for Christmas." Two new songs were added: "One Bright Star," written by John Jarvis, and "Til' the Season Comes Around Again," by Jarvis and Randy Goodrum. If you haven't heard Vince's velvet voice and great playing on these beautiful songs, well, you know what to do.

On the ever-popular "Santa Claus Is Coming to Town," Vince shows off his great guitar pickin' in a fully instrumental, Chet Atkins and Les Paul–style version that convinces you Santa Claus is stoppin' at the dance hall (or maybe even the honky tonk!) before he climbs down your chimney. He gives a similar treatment to the Irving Berlin classic "White Christmas," mostly playing the song and singing the famous chorus only once. You can hear the words, though, because the way Vince plays, it's like the guitar is singing them.

One of the nicest treats on this holiday collection is the title song. On "Let There Be Peace on Earth," a song sung in many churches and written by Sy Miller and Jill Jackson, Jenny Gill sings a duet with her father. Her sweet young voice shows there really is that blood connection in vocal power.

> "What was neat about it was that I started to understand what my mom and dad feel when they see me do something good. It's an amazing feeling."
>
> —VINCE GILL

Vince said he and Jenny sang the song a few times through and that he was overwhelmed when he heard what they sounded like. "It's the neatest thing I've ever done," he said.

Vince had been working on the Christmas album when his brother died back in March. "It Won't Be the Same This Year," the last song on the album, tells the story of someone going home for the first Christmas after his brother has passed away. The stockings are hung and the Christmas carols are sung, but without him it just won't be the same. Vince wrote the song himself and it is a haunting, achingly beautiful celebration of family and love.

One of the most gratifying things for artists is to have the opportunity to create something lasting and meaningful for the people they love best. "My family will have something that means a lot," he said after completing the album. "While it was a story about my brother, a lot of people will relate to the same emotions."

In early 1994, Janis Gill talked about the need for an artist to spend long periods of time on the road. She told the *Nashville Tennessean* that for herself and Vince, "the two-career deal is a comfort. I know how hard it is on the road. I know exactly what he has to go through, and he understands the same when Kristine and I are out." She said it really helped to understand what the other was going through.

Around the same time, Vince told a newspaper that he was finding a lot of joy in the simpler things in life. Instead of going to find new records and spending hours listening to them, "I can go to the movies with my kid and have a hot dog. The parameters are different now than when I was eighteen years old."

True. Now, he was a star.

CHAPTER EIGHT

Giving Something Back

"I guess I have something of a reputation for being a golf nut. What can I say? Guilty as charged."

—VINCE GILL

Ever since he was in the third grade and began playing golf with his dad, Vince Gill had been a real, to use his word, nut about the sport. Vince has said his dad wasn't a great golfer, "but he got me started and I didn't let go."

"It's my passion. When I get out there, it's something totally different from country music." The normally serene and laid-back Vince Gill becomes a different person on the golf course. He has a drive to play well, just as he does with music. "But I'm not out there for a little walk in the park," he said. "I'm out there to beat a course to its knees. Golf is one constant I'll keep for the rest of my life."

Even his temper comes out. "People are surprised because I seem so goofy and easygoing," he said. "But I've been known to break a golf club and use every curse word."

Vince isn't alone in his passion for golf. What used to be the sport of upper-class businessmen in private country clubs has, over the last decade or so, attracted men and women from every walk of life. In Nashville, it's a joke that more country music business is conducted on the area's many golf courses than on Music Row.

At one point it was reported that Vince Gill played golf every day that the temperature was over forty-five degrees and he wasn't working. He has memberships at four clubs in Nashville, another two outside the state, and is a semi-regular at PGA pro-ams. "I can shoot anywhere from sixty-eight to eighty-eight on any given day," he says.

Of course, when he's working, he devotes himself to his music. "These last few years have been so crazy," he said. "Finding time to play has been difficult. Tour schedules have been so crazy that I'm worn out. It's real hard to make myself go out there and beat balls. But the clubs are always there."

Did he ever wonder what it might have been like to be Vince Gill, pro golfer? "Sure, I'd love to know what I could have accomplished if I'd hit five hundred balls a day from age sixteen to twenty-four," he said. "I honestly ask myself if I had enough talent to play the tour. I might have had enough talent to have gotten a card, but I don't know if I had enough talent to go out there and win. I really think I made a wise decision."

Do golf and singing have anything in common? "I think both require great mechanics and imagination. You can have great mechanics as a singer or guitar player," he said, "but if you don't have the creativity and soul and things like that, it's likely you won't reach the top level. Same with golf."

A reporter once asked Vince which was more exciting: getting a hole in one or winning Entertainer of the Year. Vince said that the hole in one was more exciting—"It's something that I had waited my entire life for"—and that winning Entertainer of the Year was more surprising. One time Vince made a hole in one at a benefit tournament. It resulted in a lucky couple winning a brand-new home!

On one of his concert tours, the laminated pass that the staff is given for security and access purposes said, "The Golfer Formerly Known as Vince."

"The more I get the more I feel I want to give."
                                              —VINCE GILL

Vince Gill's generosity as a musician is no secret. From the start of his career, he was always willing to lend his voice and guitar skills to the work of his friends and colleagues. There was even a point where he was warned that he could become overexposed as a musician by being heard on so many records so often, but that didn't stop him. The guy loves to sing and play, and there are countless artists who will tell you they are always thrilled and honored to have Vince on their albums.

One of the other qualities that has given Vince Gill his reputation as "the nicest guy in Nashville" is his genuine devotion to charity work. He lends his talents to many albums like *Mama's Hungry Eyes*, a Merle Haggard tribute album that benefits the Second Harvest Food Bank. He spends time with the children in the Make-A-Wish Foundation program. He is a big part of Fan Fair's annual Celebrity Softball Game. The list of charities that have benefited from Vince's generosity is long.

"I think what I do is very simple," he says of his efforts. "If going somewhere and singing a song or playing some music can help, I'll do it. That's nothing." Though he gets a lot of press for his charity work, that's not the motivation. "I don't have to get a lot of press," he said. "I have also played in small tournaments that raised $10,000 for good causes.

"What I do is a piece of cake," he said. "I show up and I sing, I show up and I play golf—and I do that every day. That's all I know how to do. All it is is time."

Kix Brooks of the reigning CMA Country Duo Brooks & Dunn says, "When I'm so worn out from riding the bus after a tour, I feel like all I can do is go to sleep. Then I'll turn on the TV and there's Vince out there, after his own tour, doing something else for the community. It's amazing."

"Vince has always been a jewel," says Trisha Yearwood. "He'll do anything for anybody."

Rick Shipp, who handles Vince's concert bookings as head of the Nashville office of the William Morris Agency said, "We're certainly ready to help Vince in any endeavor, but we admire and respect the fact that he is willing to give so much time and effort to charities, and we fully support him in those efforts."

When Vince won the Minnie Pearl Award at the TNN/Music City News Awards in 1993 in recognition of his humanitarianism, he said, "I'm more proud of that one than any other award."

In 1993, Vince Gill decided to have a small golf party. He thought he'd invite several tour golfers to Nashville for a little golf and a little music to benefit the Tennessee PGA Junior Tour. His interest in the idea grew out of his recognition of golf as a positive influence on his own youth.

Vince Gill's Favorite Charities

The Relief Fund/The Red Cross
(Oklahoma City Bombing)

T. J. Martell Foundation

The Vinny Pro-Celebrity Golf Invitational

The Ear Foundation

Belmont University

Make-A-Wish Foundation

"Lose Your Blues" Perry Ellis promotion for
the National Coalition for the Homeless

Easter Seals

Feed the Children

Sara Lee Classic

"If kids had something to do, something to oc-
cupy their time, they wouldn't get in trouble. It
doesn't matter if it's golf or basketball or baseball or art."

—VINCE GILL

That little get-together raised $50,000. It has since be-
come one of the biggest events of the year in Nashville,
and it goes by the name of The Vinny. Each year it has
grown tremendously.

The first day of The Vinny features stars of the PGA, the

Mercy Homes

Baptist Hospital—Nashville

Waldon Pond Project (Rain Forest Fund)
with the Eagles

The Jimmy Everest Cancer Center

Special Care (Children's Disabilities)

Pregnancy Crisis Center—Nashville

American Heart Association

Mama's Hungry Eyes

UMC Children's Pediatric Intensive Care Unit

Cerebral Palsy Foundation

Kidney Foundation

Senior PGA, and the LPGA tours competing for a $65,000 purse. The second day belongs to the celebrities, including top country and pop music entertainers, TV and movie stars, and sports figures. And, of course, Vince himself.

Over the years, The Vinny has attracted some of the biggest names in the entertainment and sports worlds. Pro golfers who have played include John Daly, Fuzzy Zoeller, Loren Roberts, Jim Furyk, Tommy Tolles, Kris Tschetter, Lanny Wadkins, and Mark McCumber. Sports stars like Rick Pitino, Don Mattingly, and Baseball Hall of Famers Johnny Bench and Brooks Robinson have also joined in. Celebrities include Garth Brooks, Reba

McEntire, Lorrie Morgan, Suzy Bogguss, Glen Campbell, Gary Chapman, Amy Grant, Mark Collie, Kix Brooks, John Michael Montgomery, Billy Dean, and more.

"I am thrilled with the support and the enthusiasm we've received from our sponsors, the community, and people around the country," Vince says.

In 1994, Janis Gill hosted a Sweetheart Luncheon and Fashion Show as part of The Vinny. "I am thrilled to host this event," she said. "I'm not a golfer, but I sure do love clothes."

At the 1995 Vinny, Vince said he was sometimes a bit uncomfortable about displaying his golf abilities in public. This from the guy who is so comfortable getting up and singing in front of tens of thousands of people. "It's extremely unnerving," he said. "When you get out of your element, that's when people start to get uncomfortable and insecure." He added another concern. "You realize you could potentially bean somebody and really hurt 'em."

The Vinny takes place at the Golf Club of Tennessee in Kingston Springs, about thirty miles west of Nashville. The funds provide and support new junior golf programs and create an endowment to support future programs. Other programs that help youth from all walks of life across the state, including scholarships for at-risk youth to the TPGA Junior Golf Academy at the Golf House of Tennessee, also benefit from The Vinny. Some money has also gone into the junior facilities at Golf House as well as the Little Course at Aspen Grove in nearby Franklin, Tennessee. The facility includes the Vince Gill Putting Green.

In March 1997, the Tennessee PGA Junior Tour was re-named the Vince Gill Tennessee PGA Junior Tour in recognition of Vince's ongoing and enormous contributions. By 1997, The Vinny had raised over $1 million. "I am especially grateful to have my name associated with kids playing golf in Tennessee, opportunities for the best players and introductions to those youngsters who have never played," Vince said. The National Golf Foundation reported that junior play in 1997 increased 33.8 percent over 1996. Vince said he was proud to have played a role in supporting junior golf.

Lissa Horton, the director of Tennessee PGA Junior Golf, said, "Vince not only supports the PGA Junior Tour monetarily, he also supports these kids with his time. We felt he should be recognized."

> "I'm glad my dad got to see this place and the green named for me. He was very happy. It was special."
>
> —VINCE GILL

Although many entertainers of Vince Gill's stature will lend their names and have their photos taken for charity events, Vince shows up at even the smallest of junior clinics. He stops by the Golf House of Tennessee in the summer to mingle with students at the Golf Academy, playing or just hanging out. He devotes an entire day in the fall hosting The Mini Vinny, a Vinny/Kid Zone–sponsored tournament for ages eight to twelve. When Nashville's daily newspaper, the *Tennessean*, held a "Visit with Vince" contest in July 1995, the winner was a ten-year-old girl from nearby Franklin who met with Vince at the Little Course at Aspen Grove. One August day in 1996, he sat on the back porch at the Golf House and, while players and sponsors picked up their credentials, he spent time with forty-eight young golfers. He autographed every cap they gave him. "I see myself in every one of these kids out there carrying their golf bags," he said.

"His time and devotion have just been incredible," said Dick Horton, executive director of the Tennessee PGA. "He is hands-on. He genuinely loves kids and golf."

"I never dreamed The Vinny would grow to this magnitude," Vince said. "Everywhere I go, fans are always asking about The Vinny."

Golf isn't the only thrill that fans get from Vince Gill during The Vinny. He also plays a concert at Nashville's beautiful Starwood Amphitheatre as part of the event. His hometown neighbors get a full taste of the many wonderful sides of Vince Gill.

> "Gill's best work to date . . . a musical portrait that details the singer's many sides and shades of love."
>
> —*Houston Chronicle*

Vince Gill's fourth MCA album, *When Love Finds You,* was getting him plenty of attention in 1994 from some of the most important media in entertainment. *People* magazine called its songs "mournful, understated ballads about heartbreak, sung in a pure quavering voice . . . not since Smokey Robinson's Motown heyday has an artist created such gorgeous rhapsodies of remorse." According to *Entertainment Weekly*, Vince Gill was using his "elastic, angelic tenor" and "soulful, hotshot guitar playing" to create a new sound. "Gill seems acutely aware of how things change in the blink of an eye," the review said. "He turns away from his bluegrass-country-pop base to experiment with white boy r&b and an understated contemporary Christian sound."

Produced by Tony Brown, the album is rich in the songs of heartache Vince has become known for. From the first notes of the first song, Vince Gill fans were gasping their delight at a whole new level of aching passion. "Whenever You Come Around," written by Vince with Pete Wasner, resonates with the shimmering emotion everyone has felt at that first realization of how far gone in love you are with someone. As the lyrics describe those weak knees, the shortness of breath, and the tongue-tied silence, Vince sings straight from the heart. On background vocals he is joined by Trisha Yearwood.

Fortunately, love finally does find the singer in "When Love Finds You," co-written by Vince and Michael Omartian, the Grammy-winning artist, songwriter, and producer who had produced records for such mega-stars as Michael Bolton, Cher, Donna Summer, Rod Stewart, and Whitney Houston. This is a song about someone who knows how it feels to be in love and can articulate it in two verses and a chorus without a wasted word. Billy Thomas, Jeff White, and Vince layer background vocals to sound like a full choir.

"Maybe Tonight" is a special song for several reasons. It has a full, rich sound, aided once again by the background vocals of Billy Thomas, Jeff White, and Vince himself. Its beautiful lyrics are filled with hope about a close friendship and long-smoldering attraction finally blooming into real love. But what makes it most notable is that it was the first song co-written by Vince and Janis Gill.

"It's the story of how we met through music and were friends before we ever started hanging out together,"

Vince told a reporter. "But when we first met, there was this little spark." He added with a smile, "I had a bigger spark than she did."

Musically, the instrumental tracks on "Maybe Tonight" can serve as a primer for how to produce a perfect record. All the instruments are in proportion and you can hear each one individually. They achieve the primary purpose of any instrumental track—to surround the singer and the lyrics as the setting surrounds a precious gem in a piece of jewelry.

Vince wrote "Which Bridge to Cross (Which Bridge to Burn)" with the legendary singer and songwriter "Whisperin' Bill"Anderson, who had earned his nickname from his relaxed, conversational vocal style. From the 1950s through the '80s, Anderson had written thirty-seven Top Ten hits, beginning with "City Lights," a number-one hit for Ray Price, and continuing with many others for such stars as Connie Smith, Lefty Frizzell, and Roger Miller. When country went pop in the early '80s, Anderson lost his record deal but continued to perform his old hits on the Grand Ole Opry radio show and on tour. Steve Wariner took Anderson's 1960 hit, "The Tips of My Fingers," to Number 3 in 1992. "Which Bridge" is a great collaboration between Vince and Bill, a beautiful and evocative waltz with a stirring sentiment.

In "A Real Ladies' Man," Vince Gill and Carl Jackson, songwriters, get even more specific on the subject of infidelity. The two verses are lyrical portrayals of an old story—out cheatin' on Saturday night, in church repenting on Sunday morning. Alison Krauss adds her unique voice to background vocals with Vince. Stuart Duncan's fiddle solo makes this a real country classic.

Another touching sentiment is voiced in "If There's

Anything I Can Do," written by Vince and John Barlow Jarvis. Vince sings of the sadness and sorrow in a friend's face and, in the tradition of such great pop hits as Carole King's "You've Got a Friend," promises to be there to help. The Doobie Brothers' former lead singer Michael McDonald adds his incomparable voice to Vince's for the background vocals.

Vince wrote "If I Had My Way" with Amy Grant, whom he called "one of the great human beings we have on this planet." It wasn't a message song, he said, "just the expression of the point of view, 'If I had my way, we'd love one another.' " Billy Thomas and Vince do background vocals.

But *When Love Finds You* also had its lighter side, and here is where Vince showed he could rock and party with the best of them. With Reed Nielsen, Vince wrote "You Better Think Twice." It's about a guy warning one of his female pals to be careful giving her heart to his best friend, a guy who just isn't going to settle down. (How many women wish they'd gotten that advice?) Billy Thomas and Nashville studio vocal legend Jonell Mosser add to the heartfelt and spirited background vocals. "South Side of Dixie," written with Delbert McClinton, is like a ride in a convertible with your best buddies down Interstate 65 from the bluegrass state of Kentucky to the Gulf shore of Alabama. Your foot's on the pedal, the top is down, and the radio's turned up. It's a guys' song that extols the charms of southern ladies.

Reed Nielsen co-wrote with Vince another rollicking song on the album. "What the Cowgirls Do" is a tribute to the cowgirls of America who love to party, not only the ones in Texas and Oklahoma but all of 'em "from Baton Rouge to Bangor, Maine." It's easy to see why this song was a hit in dance clubs as well as on radio—it's as much fun as a night out, jumping from beer joint to honky tonk until dawn. If you can listen to this song and not tap your feet, maybe you need a vacation. Vince, as usual, turns in an exceptional guitar solo here and Billy Thomas's background vocals add to the fun.

The video for "What the Cowgirls Do" features Vince Gill fronting a band consisting of his manager Larry Fitzgerald on stand-up bass, producer and friend Tony Brown on keyboards, renowned bass player Willie Weeks on drums, Grand Ole Opry favorite Little Jimmy Dickens on acoustic guitar, and Vince's old friend songwriter and musician Rodney Crowell on fiddle. But the most fun is seeing Calvert DeForest, who is known to fans of "Late Night with David Letterman" as Larry "Bud" Melman, wowing the assembled listeners with his fancy footwork, doing as silly a Texas two-step as has ever graced a dance floor. Vince may be the cute musician playing his guitar, but as the video ends, it's DeForest who's in the back of a pickup truck frolicking with the cowgirls and it's Vince behind the wheel as the chauffeur.

When Love Finds You spawned an incredible six hit singles. More than a celebration of the power of love, Vince Gill's music was now contemplating how to make the right choices in life and affirming the need to express love to people while you still have them around. This album sees Vince Gill's longtime collaboration with Tony Brown really hitting its stride. There are incredible performances and a technically flawless production. (On every song, by the way, Vince's old pal Randy Scruggs, son of bluegrass legend Earl Scruggs, lends his guitar stylings.) Here is a Vince Gill totally comfortable with himself as a writer and performer—an artist at the top of his game.

From the song choices to the guitar solos, Vince has truly arrived as an artist who can contend with anyone in any genre of music.

At the BMI dinner in 1994, held during CMA Awards week, Vince Gill was again named Songwriter of the Year. He said this award meant more to him than any other. It had to do with the song.

The song—the last cut on *When Love Finds You*—had done a lot for Vince in helping him deal with something sad. It was "Go Rest High on That Mountain."

Vince had been pleasantly surprised that MCA had released it as a single to stores. He always saw his role as the artist, recording the songs he wanted the way he wanted them recorded, but when it came to the actual marketing of his albums, he left it all up to MCA. "When they released it, I was really excited because I know how positive that song is," he said. He felt the song was musically strong and had a lot of spirituality to it. He wondered how radio would react and whether it would get a lot of airplay.

> "Probably of any song I've written, this one means more to me than anything because it's so personal."
>
> —VINCE GILL

Vince had begun "Go Rest High on That Mountain" soon after Keith Whitley died in 1989. Whitley had gone from being a bluegrass prodigy to success as a vocalist in the late 1980s with hits like "When You Say Nothing at All" and "I'm No Stranger to the Rain," which became the 1989 CMA Single of the Year. He was married to singer Lorrie Morgan, who wrote of their life together in her 1997 book *Forever Yours, Faithfully*. Vince didn't finish the song at the time because he didn't want anyone to think he was taking advantage of what had happened to his friend. But when his brother died in March 1993, Vince turned back to the song and finished it. "I brought it back out because I needed to deal with this emotion," he said.

The emotion gives rise to a strong message of hope that those who leave us too early can find some measure of rest in a better place, the rest and peace they couldn't find here for whatever reason. Vince said writing and performing the song really helped him deal with losing people he loved. But he didn't just write it for himself. "Even though 'Go Rest High' is extremely personal," Vince said, "there isn't anybody that listens to it that can't make it pertain to them in some way. It's amazing the impact that it's having."

It was only natural that Vince would ask Ricky Skaggs and Patty Loveless to join him for background vocals on the song. They make the song sound like a country church choir. Like Keith Whitley, they are both Kentuckians and, like Vince's brother, they are both close to Vince.

"Go Rest High on That Mountain" joins other Vince Gill songs as anthems about real life that will live on as classic country music songs of the 1990s. This song—like "Amazing Grace," the Beatles' "Yesterday," and Tony Arata's composition for Garth Brooks, "The Dance"—is destined to be played at memorials for decades to come.

Up on the podium once again hosting the 1994 CMA Awards, Vince was having a great evening. Then it got even better when he made music business history by winning Top Male Vocalist for the fourth time. "I'm so thankful to be part of it," Vince said. "I won't take it lightly. I'll treat you with class."

He was also one of several country artists who shared the honors for Album of the Year for *Common Thread: The Songs of the Eagles*. This superb album features Nashville's top artists singing their own versions of such major hits from the California band as "Lyin' Eyes," "Best of My Love," "Heartache Tonight," "Take It to the Limit," and many others. Vince does a soulful version of "I Can't Tell You Why." *Common Thread* celebrated the phenomenon Vince had seen in L.A.—the coming together of long-hair California music and short-haired country. Proceeds went in part to help save land near Henry David Thoreau's retreat at Walden Pond.

Just to make the evening even more exciting, Vince won his second Entertainer of the Year award.

After the CMAs, Stan Gill, Vince's father, told *People* magazine he had recognized Vince's musical gift when his son was young. "I didn't doubt his talent, but frankly I didn't expect him to gain the success he has."

> "He'll go down in the basement and blast his CDs."
>
> —JENNY GILL

> "I think I'm the only man in captivity whose daughter screams at him, 'Turn that thing down!' "
>
> —VINCE GILL

Vince was back at the Opry House in January 1995 to help George and Barbara Bush celebrate their fiftieth wedding anniversary. Staying at the presidential suite at the Opryland Hotel, the former president and first lady were once again affirming their love of country music.

The guests included all five of the Bushes' children and their husbands and wives as well as Delta Burke and her husband, Gerald McRaney. The Oak Ridge Boys, big favorites of the Bushes, were on hand to entertain as were Ricky Skaggs, Lee Greenwood, Loretta Lynn, and Charlie Daniels. The show, entitled "With Love, From Nashville," was taped and later aired on The Nashville Network.

Vince said the state of the Bushes' union was "pretty impressive," and added, "They have a way of making you feel like their kid."

He went back to the Opryland Hotel in February when he was honored as Tennessean of the Year at the annual Tennessee Sports Hall of Fame. Just a few months earlier he had been named the 1994 Kiwanis Club Outstanding Nashvillian for his involvement in music and humanitarian causes. The prestigious award had previously been given to Roy Acuff, Minnie Pearl, and Nashville mayor Phil Bredesen. "I'm really thankful that the people of Tennessee have accepted me as one of their own," Vince said.

From there, he went on to kick off his 1995 national tour in Cleveland, Ohio, to a capacity crowd at the Cleveland State University Convocations Center with a three-hour show that one observer called "a marriage of American musical styles that is the hallmark of the best contemporary country." Vince's show was a marathon of nearly thirty songs blending traditional country with everything from rock, pop, and soul to gospel, blues, and r&b.

He performed on a stage set that another reviewer called "probably the cleverest set on the country concert circuit." Paying homage to all the American kids who'd been in a "garage band" in high school (no doubt because their parents wouldn't let them play in the house), Vince Gill's set had paint cans, boxes of junk, and a speed-limit sign that said 33 1/3. (For those of you too young to remember, that's the speed of a long-playing record prior to CDs and tapes.) There was even a basketball hoop and a weather vane—and a fake aluminum door that opened at the start of the show.

Writing for the *Cleveland Plain Dealer*, Michael Norman said Vince "gave the mostly female audience plenty of reason to sway and swoon" with his many romantic ballads. The audience especially loved his rendition of "The Heart Won't Lie" with backup singer Dawn Sears singing the parts Reba sang when Vince recorded the song with her.

Later in February, Vince played the biggest party in Texas, the famed Houston Livestock Show and Rodeo. The annual eighteen-day extravaganza attracts hundreds of thousands of visitors from all over the United States and the world. It begins with the Downtown Rodeo Parade featuring dozens of floats, several marching bands, and thousands of trail riders, all of whom travel along more than twenty-four blocks lined with crowds of cheering spectators. These same crowds pack the World Championship Bar-B-Contest to sample the lip-smacking best recipes of cooks from all over the great state of Texas. The Rodeo Fireworks Spectacular has been called the best fireworks display anywhere in America.

The biggest attraction of the Houston Livestock Show and Rodeo, in the opinion of country music fans, is the amazing lineup of country music stars who appear nightly throughout the event at the Houston Astrodome. The folks who attend this event are accustomed to seeing Vince Gill on stage—after all, he first played here as an opening act in 1983. But on that February night in 1995, the more than 52,000 fans waiting for Vince were rewarded with one of the best shows they'd ever seen. Vince played all of his hits, treated the audience to a lot of western swing, and showed what a sensational guitar player he was.

Marty Racine, a reviewer for the *Houston Chronicle*, noted that although Vince Gill plays country music with the best of them, he kept a distinctive individuality in the Nashville of the 1990s. "He doesn't wear cowboy hats, western shirts, or belt buckles the size of baby armadillos," Racine wrote. "He doesn't walk like he just got off a horse, came out of a saloon, or his Wranglers received too much starch."

Next, he showed New York City what great music was all about, no matter what label you put on it. At the Paramount in Madison Square Garden in March, Vince Gill earned the praises of the *New York Times*'s popular music critic John Pareles, who said that Vince's guitar-playing "cuts loose, zooming and snaking in flawless curlicues." He also praised Vince's songwriting, saying, "his characters are fond of honky tonks but less for the chance of an illicit rendezvous than for the music."

While in New York, Vince appeared on "Live with Regis and Kathie Lee." He told the morning hosts one of the things he loved about visiting the Big Apple was the city's great pizza. "I love to go to a little place called Vinnie's," he said. It's on Manhattan's Upper West Side.

On April 19, 1995, just after nine o'clock in the morning, Central Standard Time, a bomb exploded in the Alfred P. Murrah Federal Building in downtown Oklahoma City, in what is almost the exact center of the United States. Rescuers rushed to the scene, officials began to investigate, and citizens all over the country watched in horror as television brought the images of this devastating event right into their living rooms. Over the next few days, we learned that 168 people had been senselessly killed— grandparents, fathers, mothers, and children; workers in the building; and visitors to the government offices housed there. Many more had been seriously wounded.

Vince Gill worked hard to provide aid to his Oklahoma City neighbors. In addition to all the times he went home to provide help and aid after the bombing, Vince participated in a Thank-You Celebration, held by the state Office of Volunteerism on July 4, 1995, at the Myriad Convention Center in Oklahoma City. Seventy-six days after the bombing, the event honored all the firemen, nurses, medics, police officers and federal agents, searchers and rescuers, comforters and counselors who were personally involved in the aftermath of the disaster.

Vince performed an acoustic show and told his neighbors that in the days after the bombing he'd gotten to "watch all of you roll up your sleeves and show once again what character and class the people of Oklahoma are all about."

He added, "I'm proud to be from here more than I've ever been."

The VH-1 Honors acknowledged Vince's efforts to help the people of Oklahoma City after the bombing through his raising money for the Governor's Victim and Family Relief Fund. He took his daughter Jenifer with him to the awards celebration in Los Angeles and his speech included a sweet tribute to her. She also got to have her picture taken with Boyz II Men.

Vince Gill's tour continued throughout the summer of 1995. Being on the road, getting to play your music for thousands of fans in city arenas and county fair grounds is part of what every musician loves to do. It's part of the dream of every artist trying to make it big.

The thrill of being onstage, however, only happens for a few hours each day. The rest of the time is spent taking down the stage, packing up the equipment, getting on the bus and traveling to the next town, where you set up the stage again, do a sound check, and get ready to perform. There are press interviews to do, autographs to sign, and parties backstage to meet fans who have won local radio contests. You also need to spend a little time staying in touch with the folks back home—the family and the record company. In between, you might get some sleep.

Vince did take one night off for himself in August to attend his twenty-year high school reunion, joining his friends and former Northwest Classen High School classmates in the Bricktown Ballroom in Oklahoma City. His classmates were excited that he was there. As usual, Vince downplayed his celebrity status.

"I felt like a normal guy in high school and I feel like a normal guy now," he said. He played a solo set and then jammed with the band that had been hired for the evening. He also took lots of pictures with his pals from the class of 1975.

When the concert tour wound down at the end of September, Vince returned to Nashville. He hadn't changed much on the road over the summer except for one thing: He had shaved his head.

It was a buzz cut. It was the kind of haircut they give marine recruits. His wife, it was reported, helped him cut it. His daughter reportedly screamed when she saw him. His record company was not happy. And when the fans got a look at him, letters of complaint started pouring in. Why did Vince shave his head? they all wanted to know.

"I'd been thinking about it for some time because I'm not the kind of guy who likes to mess with his hair," he said. He said he saved a fortune on shampoo and didn't need to carry a blow dryer—there were all kinds of benefits to not having a whole lot of hair. "I'm really just a rumpled kind of guy who likes to go out with his shirttail hanging out."

> "I wanted to see what my head looks like. I haven't seen it in about thirty-two years since I had a burr. I told my dad he used to make me wear it this way."
>
> —VINCE GILL

Vince had done a lot of work with the Make-A-Wish Foundation, with a lot of kids who had lost their hair as a result of chemotherapy. "They're all worried about it," he said. "I just wanted to show them, man, it's no big deal, it's the least of your worries."

He hastened to add that he had shaved it himself and saved twenty bucks.

His management company told the press that Vince is "his own man" when it comes to his image. MCA Records told him he had to grow it back because it had been deemed "unsatisfactory" ("That was the term they used," Vince said), but after telling him the official company line, Tony Brown went out and got a haircut just like Vince's.

But that was nothing compared to the reaction of the fans.

"Hey, kids. How's everybody?" When Vince took the stage at the Ryman Auditorium for a concert to be taped for broadcast on TNN and CMT, the audience gasped out loud. Not only was his hair incredibly short, he had grown a goatee and was limping due to recent knee surgery.

The show at the Ryman was an informal, acoustic concert previewing the upcoming release of Vince's greatest hits album, *Souvenirs*. It was the first time he'd ever played there for a whole night. Vince called the Ryman "the most amazing place I've ever sung in. The acoustics, the way the music reverberates and delays, is so perfect," he said. Vince told the audience there wasn't a better place to play music than the Ryman and that he and Nashville were lucky to have it. The audience cheered their agreement. They were treated to great versions of all his hits, including a terrific instrumental jam on "Liza Jane."

"If you can't dance to this one, you can't dance," Vince said as he introduced the next song, written with "my buddy Pete Wasner." It brought a cheer and a lot of bopping in the seats—"Don't Let Our Love Start Slippin' Away" is a favorite Vince Gill song for all kinds of fans.

Vince told the audience that when he was sixteen or seventeen years old, he heard a bluegrass family band called the Whites at a festival in Oklahoma. "I'd never heard singing and playing like this before and I was hooked," he said. He treated the crowd to a Whites song called "Buck's Run" that really showed off the picking skills of his whole band. These were the guys he'd been playing with for a long time—Pete Wasner on piano, Jeff White on guitar, Jimmy Johnson on bass, Billy Thomas on drums—"the way they're supposed to be played," Vince said—and Jeff Gurnsey on fiddle and mandolin. Gurnsey tore the house down with his fiddle solo on "One More Last Chance," followed by a great piano solo by Pete Wasner. Then the whole band jammed the song to the end of the show.

But wait! The crowd wanted more. Vince came back and sang his contribution to the *Common Thread* album, his favorite Eagles song. The Don Henley/Glenn Frey/Timothy B. Schmit classic "I Can't Tell You Why" sounds amazing in Vince's voice. His long, sweet guitar solo stretched the song out to over six minutes. The audience could have listened for another six minutes.

Though the show was intended to promote *Souvenirs*, "I'll tell you what," Vince said, "being in this building made me want to sing this song. We hadn't planned to sing it. This is not on the record, but I wanted to do it for you guys tonight." He said he hoped the song would be on the TV version of the concert (it was) and then sang "Go Rest High on That Mountain." Vince and his band received a standing ovation.

When the concert aired, the letters started pouring in from fans about his hair—or lack of it. Most fans wanted Vince to look like the Vince they had grown to love.

By the time of the 1995 CMA Awards, Vince's hair was growing back in, but it was still pretty short. He was hosting again and was as naturally funny as he'd always been. Awards show hosts usually have a team of writers backstage scripting funny lines in response to events that happen during the live show, but Vince didn't seem to need that. "We've tried to script humor in the past and it doesn't work as well as Vince just doing something spontaneous," said Ed Benson, the executive director of the CMA.

The short-haired Vince did win his fifth consecutive Male Vocalist of the Year award. "I'm just lucky, I guess," he said. "These awards go in cycles. I'd won four years in a row and I thought, 'Surely they're sick of me now.'"

He was especially happy that some of his closest music

colleagues won awards that night and joined in the cheering when the envelopes were opened. Patty Loveless won Album of the Year for *When Fallen Angels Fly*. No one was more excited and thrilled for her than Vince. Then his bluegrass buddy Alison Krauss won Female Vocalist of the Year, Vocal Event of the Year (with Shenandoah, for "Somewhere in the Vicinity of the Heart"), and the Horizon Award. Single of the Year (for "When You Say Nothing at All") went to Alison Krauss and Union Station.

Krauss had scored a number-one hit in 1995, harmonizing with Keith Whitley. Using modern studio technology, she sang with Whitley after his death on his hit "When You Say Nothing at All." Instead of chasing success on the radio charts, she was staying true to her bluegrass roots. Alison Krauss and Union Station are probably the most commercially successful exponents of bluegrass today. In fact, they had revitalized interest in bluegrass in the United States at a time when it was more popular in Europe and Japan.

After the CMAs, Vince went to Oklahoma City to play in his golf tournament as part of the city's annual Festival of the Horse. Then he planned to take the rest of the year off and spend time at home with his family in Nashville.

On November 14, players and fans were gathered for a basketball game at the Striplin Gymnasium on the campus of Belmont University in Nashville. Majestic old buildings on an especially beautiful campus house the university's many departments, most notably its music department, which offers studies and degrees in—what else—the music business. But this was no ordinary basketball game. The teams consisted of Vince Gill and an all-star roster of country music's most talented men and women playing in the sixth annual Vince Gill Country Music Celebrity Basketball Game and Concert. The event raises funds to be used for scholarships and program enhancements for Belmont University's athletic and music departments.

Vince had inaugurated the event in November 1990 after he served as honorary chairman of Vanderbilt's Music City Invitational Tournament.

> "Basketball is a great release for me. It's a blast. I get a great seat, plus I get to sing the anthem before fifteen thousand people. What more could anybody ask for?"
>
> —VINCE GILL

Fresh from his 1995 concert tour and the big hoo-hah over his shaved head, Vince said, "It really has been a busy year and it has cut into my golf game. But I've been able to make most of our basketball games." The men's teams competed in two twelve-minute halves. During half time a women's team made up of singer/songwriter Matraca Berg, Terri Clark, Linda Davis, Tanya Tucker, Michelle White, and Janis Gill and her sister, Kristine, played a ten-minute game.

The evening raised more than $65,000 for Belmont University. "Our goal," Vince said, "has always been to invite a few friends, have a good time, and help out a university that I believe is providing a terrific education to a lot of young people."

"Belmont University has appreciated for years the efforts of Vince and his friends to lend their names and help the athletics and music business departments of this school," said Bob Mulloy, associate dean for music business. Men's basketball coach Ricky Byrd said, "We're looking forward to working with Vince on this fund-raiser for years to come."

CHAPTER NINE

For the Music

Souvenirs was released in January 1996. A fifteen-song retrospective of Vince Gill's career from 1989 to 1995, it featured nine songs that had become number-one hits as well as comments from Vince about each track. At around the same time, RCA released a collection called *The Essential Vince Gill*, twenty songs from 1983 to 1988, the years he spent on that label. One journalist said about the RCA collection, "the set proves that Gill was firmly in place long before he struck it big."

In talking about *Souvenirs* and what it meant to have such a stellar body of work, Vince said, "I can't put a finger on it except to say that record to record, I've always felt like I've gotten better and made progress. That, to me, was the exercise. Still is."

What *Souvenirs* showed best was that Vince Gill had centered his choices and decisions around the songs themselves, on maintaining respect for the music. "We never tried to tone something down if we felt like it should have been, say, r&b leaning," he said. "And if the music felt real, real country, we didn't try to make it slicker or more pop."

Country Weekly agreed. "Gill seems almost too good to be true," the magazine wrote. "But he's the real deal when

it comes to country, deftly matching his traditional roots
with just enough contemporary touches to appeal to longtime fans and curious newcomers."

> "She's a great part of my past . . . when she
> asked me to sing that song with her, I immedi-
> ately said I would."
>
> —VINCE GILL

Dolly Parton—just saying her name makes every lover
of country music smile. The amazing star who went from
an impoverished upbringing in the Smoky Mountains of
east Tennessee to the very top of the country music world
has written some truly wonderful songs. One of her best
had been a hit first for Dolly from the movie *The Best
Little Whorehouse in Texas* and then a big smash for
Whitney Houston's *The Bodyguard*. Even LeAnn Rimes
put it out—on her first independently produced album
when she was only eleven years old. Now Dolly was
asking Vince Gill to sing it with her for her new album.

The song, of course, is "And I Will Always Love You."
Vince Gill was only too happy to oblige. After recording
the song, Vince said the experience was "tremendous because Dolly is such a jewel. That song has been a hit three
times already. I just hope I don't break the string." The
duet was included on Dolly's album *Something Special*.

Now, when artists decide to do something together for
fun and for the music, there shouldn't be any problem. But
when two artists are signed to big, powerful record companies, those companies have to be involved in all of their
artistic decisions. Vince had had some legal tussles once
with record companies back in the early 1980s, when he
and Rosanne Cash had recorded "If It Weren't for Him."

Now a similar conflict was occurring again. MCA Records agreed that Vince could do the duet with Dolly only if it were an album cut and not a single. This was partly because MCA was releasing "Go Rest High on That Mountain" as a single during that same period and they didn't want the two songs to compete. But Vince didn't want to restrict Dolly's use of the song.

"I would love to see Dolly Parton have another hit on the radio again," he said. "Her voice is just as great as it always was." So he went to MCA and persuaded them to let her use the duet as a single after "Go Rest High on That Mountain" had run its course.

The problem was that the song turned out really well. When Dolly's album came out, radio stations started playing the duet cut. Listeners loved it. Vince was happy the song was getting attention.

The only way to keep the song off the radio would have been for MCA and Vince Gill to take legal action against Sony to force them to withdraw the song even though country radio wanted it. This was the last thing Vince wanted to happen.

"After we recorded it, I really had a hard time with the arrogance of saying it can't be a single," he said. "I said, let's just ask everybody to live in a perfect world for three months and see if both records can be hits. There's no reason they can't because they're different and they're both great songs." When the two songs appeared on *Billboard*'s charts, one right on top of the other, Vince felt that was okay. He said he just wanted to do "the right thing, the honorable thing, the musical thing" and didn't want politics or egos or business concerns to dictate what should happen to creativity.

Vince's dad, Stan Gill, saw him perform the duet with

Dolly. "He got to have his photo taken with her," Vince said. "He's not even looking at the camera. He has the biggest grin on his face."

When the Grand Ole Opry reached its seventieth birthday, it was time for Nashville to throw broadcasting's longest-running program a big old country party.

"The Grand Ole Opry 70th Anniversary Celebration" began by taking a look back at the roots of honky tonk music and western swing, honoring Ernest Tubb, Lefty Frizzell, Loretta Lynn, and Hank Williams Sr. Hank Williams Jr. and Alan Jackson performed Hank Williams's classic "Mind Your Own Business." Patty Loveless paid a loving tribute to Emmylou Harris and the two sang Harris's song "Even Cowgirls Get the Blues." Barbara Mandrell, Chet Akins, and singer/songwriter Don Gibson collaborated on "Oh Lonesome Me," a prime example of the so-called Nashville sound, created by Atkins and Gibson, which dominated country music for twenty years.

A segment on the Opry's greatest stars acknowledged Country Music Hall of Fame and Opry legend George Jones as the ultimate country singer. Roy Clark and Mike Snider did a special rendition of "Mountain Dew" and Little Jimmy Dickens sang the colorful "Out Behind the Barn," followed by a loving tribute to Opry comedienne Minnie Pearl as the ladies of the Grand Ole Opry sang Pearl's favorite song, "Have I Told You Lately That I Love You." Through the magic of technology, Lorrie Morgan sang an emotional duet with her late father, Opry star George Morgan, of his song "Candy Kisses," the last song performed at the Ryman in 1974 before the Grand Ole Opry was moved out to Opryland.

Opry member Vince Gill was a part of the celebration,

too. He sang bluegrass great Bill Monroe's signature song "Blue Moon of Kentucky" and played in an all-star bluegrass band with Ricky Skaggs, Marty Stuart, Pam Tillis, and Mark O'Connor. Then a seven-foot statue of Bill Monroe, to be permanently displayed at the Opry, was unveiled.

After *Souvenirs*, the musician in Vince craved something new. "After *Souvenirs*, I think there was an element of starting a new chapter," he said.

"It was time to reinvent ourselves and do something a little different. . . . I wanted to shake the tree a little bit."

—VINCE GILL

Vince Gill's fans wouldn't have minded if he'd just gone on giving them more great country ballads like "When I Call Your Name," "Never Knew Lonely," "I Still Believe in You," and all the others they'd grown to count among their favorite songs. Listeners who'd tapped their feet to great upbeat country hits like "Liza Jane," "One More Last Chance," and "What the Cowgirls Do" would have welcomed ten more tunes just like them.

But true artists need to mix up the paints a little differently every now and then. They need to listen to what their inner muse is telling them and expand a little to satisfy themselves. An artist like Vince Gill, with so many roots in so many different fertile soils of musical background, needs to stretch himself in new directions.

"I want to push the envelope again," he said. "I want to create some different musical feels, especially on the songs with tempo. Not that there are any new feels, but there are new ones for me." He said he wanted to experiment a little and go a little farther than being Vince Gill the country guitar player. Instead, he said, he wanted to try to play like Mark Knopfler or Eric Clapton. He wanted to try playing a song that had, maybe, a New Orleans feel. "I love all that stuff," he said.

"I really enjoy seeing my records be extreme," he said, "like on the last album where there's something as pop-ish as 'When Love Finds You' and then something as hardcore country as 'Which Bridge to Cross.' For some reason, which is a lucky reason for me, they both work."

Now he wanted to go even farther in new directions. "Tony Brown and I made four records together, and I think we improved each record, which is obviously what you're trying to accomplish, but then it's like, OK, let's do something different than we've ever done."

Vince also wanted to see if he could write some songs by himself. Because there's so much co-writing in Nashville, Vince often started a song and then held it for another writer to finish. Now he wanted to see if he could start and finish a song by himself. Guess what? He could.

So with five new songs that he'd written alone, and five more new songs he co-wrote, Vince Gill released his new album in May 1996. It was called *High Lonesome Sound*. It had been a long time since Vince Gill's last studio album and a lot of people were waiting for this new one. Vince joked, "I've been telling people that it's been so long in between because I didn't have enough hair to shoot an album-cover picture."

The title was the phrase Bill Monroe had originated to describe the singular sound of bluegrass music. It was no accident that Vince wanted to give his thanks to Monroe, who had been hospitalized with a stroke in 1996. "This is a real tribute to him," Vince said. "He's one of the strongest men that's ever been."

The album included two versions of the title track—one an electric bluegrass feel, the other a traditional bluegrass acoustic version featuring Alison Krauss and Union Station. Krauss contributed her vocals to each song.

Vince said that Alison's success was a real breakthrough and maybe helped him feel more comfortable about making a record like *High Lonesome Sound*.

"The strange thing is, when you used to talk to other musicians, they were always interested in bluegrass and traditional country. None of us ever lost interest."

—VINCE GILL

The lyrics and the melody in "High Lonesome Sound," written by Vince, harking back to his days with Sundance, are timeless, classic bluegrass. It could have been written thirty years ago, and thirty years from now somebody will rediscover this song and call it a bluegrass classic.

The electric version of "High Lonesome Sound" was released to radio but didn't do well. Vince said, "I thought it was a really unique record. I thought it had a neat feeling with banjo and a kind of Stevie Wonder keyboard playing a 'Superstition' groove underneath it, with fiddles and twangy guitars." Vince also felt the song was "a cross between Bill Monroe and Stevie Wonder." He wasn't angry that it didn't make it on radio. He'd long enjoyed a great friendship with country radio programmers and his songs had always performed well. So country radio was willing to give the song a try. Maybe it was just too different from the usual Vince Gill fare even though the musicianship and the performance are superior.

"Just when you thought Gill had settled permanently into a comfortable, can't miss formula . . . he puts what wasn't broke on the block for a major fix," wrote *Guitar Player* magazine. "The best evidence of his ability to shine in varied settings is found in the two versions of the title cut."

People magazine's Ralph Novak also praised *High Lonesome Sound.* "A lively, melodious album," he wrote. "Gill has positioned himself as one of Nashville's most consistent performers, turning out one solid album after another."

"One Dance with You" is, in Vince's words, "a kind of roadhouse blues shuffle, not unlike Stevie Ray Vaughan or B. B. King, that kind of blues styling in the guitar playing." Vince wrote this one with Reed Nielsen. The background vocalists include Vince, Robert Bailey, Billy Thomas, and Chris Rodriguez.

"A lot of people will argue that you can't sing a song unless you've lived through it—and there may be some truth to that," Vince said, "but I believe that you don't have to live blue in order to sing blue."

The result of Vince's sorrow over the tragic drive-by shooting of a little Nashville girl is the song "Pretty Little Adriana." "I saw the news on TV and it moved me," he said. "Her pretty name, her picture, her smile, and she was about Jenny's age. I wrote it from a parent's point of view." The song received significant airplay and remains a part of Vince's concert repertoire. He won a Grammy for the song in 1998 and performed it on the show. When arrests were finally made in the case in the fall of 1998, the song was mentioned in the news stories.

Country goes to the city with "A Little More Love," another solo songwriting success by Vince Gill. Here he shows that like every musician of his generation, he has been influenced by the masters of pop, the Beatles. This song could as easily have been sung by Paul McCartney. Only the instrumental breaks, with his unique guitar style, are unmistakably Vince Gill. Kim Richey and Jeff White join Vince on the background vocals.

"Down to New Orleans," written with keyboard player Pete Wasner, has a Little Feat kind of feeling to it. Strong vocal background is provided by Bekka Bramlett, daughter of 1970s rockers Delaney and Bonnie, who has also sung with Fleetwood Mac and Billy Joel. Vince said choosing her to sing was "as inspired as anything I've ever done in my life." In the recording studio, there wasn't even a practice run. The first time Bekka opened her mouth, "It just blew me away," he said. "It was the most impressive studio performance I've ever heard."

It's a real credit to Tony Brown, who is not only the record's producer with creative responsibility but also the president of the record company itself with financial responsibility, to allow Vince to use every color on his palette and not to intrude in the process or impose his own musical will. Brown said the goal was to stretch the boundaries but not alienate the fans. "We tried to be a little different without changing the sound too much," he said. "Everybody likes the comfort zone of Vince sounding like Vince, but at the same time, everybody wants the new album to up those sounds a little."

Vince Gill knew some of his fans would find *High Lonesome Sound* a departure from his usual fare. But surely they understood when he said, "I really wanted to try some new things, especially with some of the up-tempo songs. I wanted to be more adventuresome in the grooves and feel of these songs. They're all different from anything I've ever done—and with them feeling as different as they do, it makes my guitar playing different."

He said that in country music, unlike rock, few songs were written around grooves. Country songwriting has always been more lyric-oriented. "Which is as it should be. I think nine times out of ten, that's what's best. But being a musician, I come with a different slant on it sometimes. We'll write around a lick or a groove instead of a title or a thought." For those of us less knowledgeable about such technical terms, a "lick" may be a series of notes, as in a guitar solo, and a "groove" may be a rhythmic or chord pattern like the guitar in "What the Cowgirls Do."

> "Instead of spending precious time trying to satisfy the country industry status quo . . . Gill dared to cut loose and feed his muse. . . . *High Lonesome Sound* is . . . the best since that career-launching album."
>
> —MARIO TARRADELL
> of the *Dallas Morning News*

MCA Nashville chairman Bruce Hinton was enthusiastic about *High Lonesome Sound*. "It's still Vince, it's still the great music you expect from him, but it has evolved. It's a fresh sound. Vince as an artist and writer continues to grow and it's really been a kick, going back to the success of *When I Call Your Name*, until now, to see each album becoming another benchmark in country music."

Some fans missed the usual Vince Gill fare and some found the new album wonderfully different and exciting.

Vince knew it was a big departure from what fans had come to expect, but he called it "a more musically satisfying album ... just me trying to have some fun." Everyone agreed that by stretching himself in new directions with more progressive arrangements, he proved again he was in it for the music.

The *Boston Globe* also endorsed Vince's new album. "There's more to Gill than ballads, as he affirms on a new disc that runs from sparse mountain bluegrass to a roadhouse rave-up reminiscent of Stevie Ray Vaughn."

High Lonesome Sound had a world premiere as unique as the album itself. A live broadcast originated from the Bluebird Cafe. During the event listeners called an 800 number to talk to Vince and his guests, including his wife, Janis, and some of the background vocalists he'd chosen to accompany him on the album. To celebrate the new album, MCA Nashville presented Vince with a handcrafted six-foot-tall oak trophy cabinet. "For a man who needs a lot of shelves, how about this for Vince," Bruce Hinton said.

Bekka Bramlett also lent her vocals to "Tell Me Lover," along with Chris Rodriguez and Robert Bailey. Vince said the song, which he wrote himself, was influenced by Sonny Landreth. "I love his guitar playing," Vince said. "He makes music that has a ton of feel." Vince had been listening to Landreth's slide guitar playing with its Bayou sound and said the music inspired him. "That's what music is supposed to do and it still does." The song is a laid-back Bayou rocker with subtle slide guitar against a live-wire electric guitar lead that underscores the vocals.

Patty Loveless once again joined Vince for the vocals on "Given More Time," which Vince wrote with Don

Schlitz. This is another trip through Louisiana in its sound and arrangement. Again, Vince and Patty go into uncharted territory and make the song sound like an old friend. "You and You Alone" is vintage Gill ("It's really an unconditional love song," Vince said) and the background vocal harmonies of Shelby Lynne and Vince add to the shimmering beauty of the sound and the sentiment.

"Worlds Apart," which Vince wrote with veteran Nashville songwriter Bob DiPiero, was the second single from the album. It was a more typical Vince Gill ballad and fared better on the radio. "I can't deny what people like best," Vince said. "And I love to sing those ballads. I know that's what made me as popular as I am. It's not my guitar playing and never was going to be my guitar playing." Still, the solo here conveys as much loss and emotion as the lyric and the voice. The full, rich sound of the song is a credit to the background vocals of Robert Bailey, Lisa Bevill, Kim Fleming, Nicole Mullen, and Chris Rodriguez.

The video for "Worlds Apart" depicts unsettling scenes of church burnings, gang violence, and social unrest. Vince was praised for branching out and giving this socially conscious depth to his lyrics.

"Jenny Dreamed of Trains" is a song Vince wrote with Guy Clark when his daughter was about two or three years old. She wanted to ride on a train. Maybe that's because in Nashville and nearby Franklin, the sound of a train whistle is heard almost every night. The song was recorded by Mary Chapin Carpenter and also by Sweethearts of the Rodeo. In the song's appearance on *High Lonesome Sound*, Jeff White joins Vince for the background vocals. By the way, Jenny got her wish when she and her parents rode a train through the Swiss Alps, a breathtakingly beautiful experience.

Vince felt he'd accomplished what he'd set out to do with *High Lonesome Sound* and felt really good about it. Having proven himself in sales, awards, and performances, he was able to branch out and do something new and different.

> "I'm fortunate that I have the luxury of experimenting. If you'd asked me two years ago what kind of record I'd make next, I wouldn't have been able to answer that."
>
> —VINCE GILL

Vince made the album at the same time he'd shaved his head. Any connection? "I've never tried to be something I'm not," he said. "But there are times when it gets a little stifling. Musically, it can be a little restrictive. Which is why I wanted to do something different with this album. I wanted to show people that I could still surprise them." The *San Diego Union* praised Vince for "stretching out artistically."

He was especially proud of all the background singers on the album. "I asked them to get involved because I thought they were the best people I could have," he said. "People like Patty Loveless and Shelby Lynne were perfect for helping me make the record I was hearing in my head." He said he felt like a casting director in a movie. "I hear a song and hear Shelby Lynne singing—or Alison, who has the purest voice."

Music City News liked the album. The reviewer wrote,

"Outstanding, remarkable, wonderful, marvelous, fabulous, spectacular, phenomenal and excellent." Whew!

High Lonesome Sound was nominated by the Country Music Association as Album of the Year.

Right up there with the CMA Awards, Fan Fair is one of country music's biggest events of the year.

More than 24,000 fans travel to Music City from all over the United States and many parts of the world to thank—and, more important to be thanked—by their favorite artists for another great year of music and fun. Only country music goes to the trouble of showing this much appreciation for the fans, whose purchase of albums and concert tickets allows so many artists to earn a living pursuing their dreams of making music. Like a colorful, down-home convention center, the exhibit halls on the state fairgrounds are lined with booths, decorated to the hilt by the artists' fan clubs, where tour information, new-album news, and lots of fun merchandise are available. The greatest moments at Fan Fair happen when the artists themselves spend time in the booth meeting and greeting the fans, who begin to line up early for their chance to shake hands with and say a few words to their favorite music makers.

The largest single organized group of visitors to Fan Fair 1996 came from Oklahoma. A travel agency in Norman organized the trip for the ninety-four members of the Sooner State, who left Oklahoma on Monday morning bound for Music City. Though one of their two buses broke down somewhere between Memphis and Nashville, they arrived with all their enthusiasm intact.

As usual, the weather during Fan Fair was hot, hot, hot. There were also a few nice thunderstorms to round out the afternoons. But rain has never dampened the excitement of being at the Tennessee State Fairgrounds, hearing hours and hours of great music and touring all the stars' booths. The chance to meet and talk with their favorite artists is what brings thousands of fans and major press organizations to Nashville every June.

"We were in line for seven and a half hours to get Vince Gill's autograph," one of the visitors from Oklahoma said. Vince was as gracious as always. He greeted all of his fans and took the time to talk to each one without rushing anyone through the line

On Tuesday night, Vince played a concert at Fan Fair. Many of the Oklahoma visitors were among the fans who were permitted to walk right close to the stage to take pictures. It was an unforgettable experience for all who attended.

In August 1996, when the Country Music Association announced its list of nominees, Vince Gill's name was called more than anyone else's. He received an unbelievable seven nominations. For the third time he was nominated for Entertainer of the Year. For the sixth time, he got a nod for Male Vocalist of the Year. Then there were nominations for Album of the Year for *High Lonesome Sound*, Vocal Event of the Year with Dolly Parton for "I Will Always Love You," and what had to be the most heartwarming and meaningful nominations of all—Single of the Year, Song of the Year, and Video of the Year for "Go Rest High on That Mountain."

In September 1996, nominees from all the musical categories performed in a concert at the Grand Ole Opry to raise money for Belmont University. What a great time to be in the audience! Where else could you hear so many great artists sing so many different kinds of music? Michael McDonald sang "What a Fool Believes." Christopher Cross sang "Sailing." From disco diva Donna Summer came "McArthur Park" and country queen Trisha Yearwood belted out her hit "Believe Me Baby, I Lied." Steven Curtis Chapman chimed in with his own special brand of contemporary Christian music and Little Texas had everyone moving to their special beat. Gary Chapman, Amy Grant, Larry Stewart, and Susan Ashton added to the musical richness. The crowd was up and dancing for the last number of the evening, Donna Summer singing her ultimate disco classic "Last Dance."

Then the Opry House got quiet. In one of those sad turns to an otherwise happy event, the news came that Bill Monroe had died that same day at the age of eighty-four of complications from a stroke. Vince ended the show by singing "High Lonesome Sound" and "Go Rest High on That Mountain," his voice breaking throughout both songs. "His legacy will finally be realized and the impact he had on music, not just bluegrass," Vince said. He compared Bill Monroe to Elvis Presley in terms of the depth of their influence, saying it would only increase as the years passed. Bluegrass inspires loyalty, he said. "Those who love bluegrass love it. It's not the style of the month."

A few days later, the men and women of country music paid their respects to the Father of Bluegrass. He lay in state in a closed casket, with his white cowboy hat on top, on the flower-covered stage of the Ryman Auditorium.

Just a few feet away from Monroe's casket, Ricky Skaggs, Marty Stuart, Roy Husky Jr., Stuart Duncan, and Vince Gill stood by holding their instruments. "If this is inappropriate," Ricky Skaggs said, "we're sorry. Pray about it and get over it." Then he and Vince and the rest of the guys launched into a rollicking version of the bluegrass standard "Rawhide."

> "I'm surprised that I still get to keep doing it. They put their trust in me because they know I have fun with it."
>
> —VINCE GILL

Once again, Vince Gill would be up on the podium, hosting the thirtieth annual Country Music Association Awards. "I just enjoy it. . . . It's the biggest night in country music. I feel like a champ that they want me to go out there and introduce folks." Looking out there and knowing every face put him at ease. "My buddies are all out there doing awful things to try to get me to goof up."

But Vince admitted he did feel a little nervous. "Because I know what it entails and how many things can go wrong," he said. "The first couple of times I was finding my way and didn't realize all the pitfalls. Now I know them all."

The evening at the Opry House on October 2 began with a stunning performance by fourteen-year-old new country sensation LeAnn Rimes singing her first huge hit, "Blue." Vince teased LeAnn when she was done, in a big brotherly fashion, and invited her to come back on stage to take another bow as the crowd cheered. LeAnn wasn't all that much younger than Vince had been when he'd started playing.

"I am just really thankful that I have accomplished what I have accomplished," he said. "I don't feel any different than when I was eighteen and left home and made $50 to pay the rent. I just play and sing."

Vince did a great job hosting, as usual. His sense of humor was very much on display. "I'm not above making fun of someone else or even myself," he said. He said he never particularly planned to do anything. "When something strikes me as funny, it's funny. If it's not, it's not. I'm just out there being me. Most people find I'm exactly the same without a camera going."

He was especially thrilled when he and Dolly Parton won Vocal Event of the Year for "I Will Always Love You." What a happy ending to the story of the two competing songs. During a commercial break, Vince walked off the stage. "I was hugging Dolly, her perfume smelled good," he said. "I was kind of in heaven and then all of a sudden people yelled 'Get out there! We're on!' I had forgotten. I ran out there and just kind of slid into the microphone." He laughed. "It ain't no biggie. It's just live television."

Song of the Year is the award given to the writer of a song. When the winner was announced, the audience roared its approval. "Go Rest High on That Mountain," Vince's beautiful tribute to Keith Whitley and to his own brother, Bob, won the prize. Vince walked out on stage to receive the award, but got only halfway to the podium before breaking down in tears, shaking his head, and just turning back.

VINCE GILL: "You want to go over to the Opry and sing a song?"
REBA McENTIRE: "Sure."

So the two of them drove the short distance to the Grand Ole Opry House and made a surprise appearance to sing their duet "The Heart Won't Lie."

Hal Durham, who later that month was retiring after years as the president of the Grand Ole Opry, paid tribute to Vince and other members of country music's younger generation of stars. "Ricky Skaggs and Vince Gill and Marty Stuart and some of these younger acts," he said, "have had the respect and feel for the Grand Ole Opry that you need if you're going to contribute to the show and be an asset to the show," he said. Durham felt the culture of the Grand Ole Opry would continue long into the future because of people like Vince and Ricky and Marty.

It was really a busy October for Vince Gill! That month he was also honored at a black tie affair by the Nashville Branch of the Arthritis Foundation. Called "A Night to Play with Vince," the reception dinner, video tribute, and presentation added Vince Gill's name to the distinguished roster of honored residents of Nashville who have made extraordinary contributions to elevate the quality of life in middle Tennessee.

"I'm my own opening act!" Vince said, as he and his band played an acoustic show featuring eight or nine of his biggest hits. Then they went backstage and changed into tuxedos.

When they returned, all dressed up, to the stage, decorated with dozens of poinsettias and twenty-foot-high Christmas trees, a symphony orchestra awaited them. "There is nothing more beautiful than being lucky enough to be able to stand and sing in front of an orchestra," Vince said. "I feel like I'm Bing Crosby, Johnny Mathis, or Nat King Cole instead of a country singer." He also noted that seeing his band in tuxedos was pretty cool, too.

Vince had wanted to do a Christmas tour for a long time, and in 1996 he got his wish. Between December 4

Vince Gill's Special Honors

1993 Minnie Pearl Award

1993 Harmony Award

1994 Tennessean of the Year
(Tennessee Sports Hall of Fame)

1994 Outstanding Nashvillian of the Year
(Kiwanis Club)

1995 VH-1 Award for efforts in
providing help to the victims of the
Oklahoma City bombing

1996 Nashville Arthritis Foundation
8th Annual Tribute Evening Award

1996 BMI Humanitarian Award

1997 Vince Gill Tennessee PGA
Junior Golf Tournament

1997 Inducted into the
Oklahoma Hall of Fame

1997 Inducted into the Oklahoma
Cowboy Hall of Fame

1997 Orville H. Gibson Lifetime
Achievement Award—Gibson Guitars

and December 15, he visited eleven cities in Minnesota, Wisconsin, Illinois, Michigan, Iowa, and Indiana to celebrate the holiday season. In each city, the local symphony and Vince's band were led by guest conductor Michael Omartian, who also performed on piano.

"Few artists inspire me like Vince," Omartian said. "I consider it an honor to be part of this concert series."

Vince Gill said the fun and enjoyment of the tour exceeded his expectations. Ticket sales were high in each city. The crowds loved his renditions of all the Christmas classics. And they choked up right along with him when he sang "It Won't Be the Same This Year." Later, Vince said that he tries to think about the funny things that happened with his brother to keep from crying when he sings the song.

For Christmas that year Vince's mother made a special present to him—she had his childhood guitar all fixed up. It still played.

As 1996 became 1997, Vince had a lot to celebrate. *High Lonesome Sound, Souvenirs,* and *When Love Finds You* were all on *Billboard*'s Top Country Albums chart. *When Love Finds You* had debuted in June 1994 and been on the chart for 130 weeks, propelled in part by "Go Rest High on That Mountain." *Let There Be Peace on Earth* had been number one for a total of twenty weeks in 1993, 1994, and 1995. In late November of both 1994 and 1995, it knocked Patsy Cline's *12 Greatest Hits* out of the number-one spot on *Billboard*'s Top Country Catalog Albums chart.

CHAPTER TEN

Full Circle

"I don't make plans, I never set goals. I like to watch it unfold. It's more of a surprise and more fun. I'd rather wait to see what happens."
—VINCE GILL

In April 1997, MCA Records hosted a party at the dramatic BMI Building on Nashville's Music Row for the friends and music industry peers of Vince Gill. Tony Brown and Bruce Hinton acknowleged Vince's successes: quadruple platinum for *I Still Believe in You*, double platinum for *When I Call Your Name*, and gold for *High Lonesome Sound*. Ed Benson, the executive director of the Country Music Association, gave Vince a specially created watercolor plaque in honor of his achievements and dedication to the CMA. Roger Sovine, vice president of BMI, presented Vince with three certificates, celebrating three songs that had been played a million times on the radio. It was the month of Vince Gill's fortieth birthday. The little boy who'd started at the age of five by learning three chords on the banjo from his father was now a superstar of country music.

The partying continued in May at the Pathmakers Lunch, an annual event sponsored by the Oklahoma City–County

Historical Society and the Greater Oklahoma City Chamber
of Commerce. The Pathmaker's Lunch honors four living
and four deceased pathmakers in Oklahoma City history.
Vince Gill had certainly done his part to honor his home
state. Also honored that day, posthumously, was Alfred P.
Murrah, an Oklahoma City federal district court judge
who ended his career as director of the Federal Justice
Center and for whom the Oklahoma City federal building
that was bombed in 1995 was named. The luncheon was
held at Applewoods Restaurant and Banquet Center, one
of the city's most popular restaurants. Usually it was quiet
outside for these events, but on that May day there were
many young girls outside the restaurant hoping to catch a
glimpse of Vince.

Throughout the summer of 1997, Vince continued to
tour, but this time with a difference. He played smaller
concert halls, places that could accommodate only a
couple of thousand people. These were really the perfect
setting for audiences to appreciate his acoustic guitar
playing and intimate vocals. It took a lot more time and effort for fans to get to see these events—keeping track of
concert announcements and getting out early to be among
the lucky few who could obtain tickets. It meant a lot to
Vince to see these fans in the audience.

The shows were called "An Evening with Vince Gill."
How about those lucky fans who got to see those shows?
What a treat. But no one enjoyed the smaller shows more
than Vince himself. "It's a blast," he said. "The shows are
real intimate. It's sometimes fun to do things you don't
normally do. I could have played a few arenas instead and
made a whole lot more money. But those fans were there
at the beginning of my career."

Vince said he always tried to play some of these smaller

places. "Actually, with my personality and sense of humor, I would rather be playing a two-hundred-seat club. It's hard to be funny and glib and come across like that in front of twelve thousand people." Of course, Vince had his share of VFW halls and bars when he was coming up. He figured he'd see them again when (and if) his popularity began to wane. "I just remember what Roy Orbison told me one time," he said. "They're all just beer joints."

Still, his 1997 tour was among the four top-grossing tours in country music that year.

Audiences and music lovers seemed to be wanting more bluegrass music and no one was more pleased to hear that than Vince Gill.

Vince had certainly made a contribution to the resurgence of interest in bluegrass with "High Lonesome Sound," which won Song of the Year honors from the International Bluegrass Music Association. His friend Alison Krauss had taken her exceptional bluegrass performance all the way to being named CMA Vocalist of the Year in 1995. Bluegrass radio was having a field day with new singles from artists not normally associated with bluegrass music. Steve Earle released an acoustic album called *Train A'Comin'* featuring many bluegrass artists. He said he'd written one song, "I Still Carry You Around," just to have something to play with the Del McCoury Band. Garth Brooks released the album *Sevens* with five songs written by bluegrass artists. Garth had acknowledged the importance of bluegrass in 1993 when his *In Pieces* album featured the New Grass Revival song "Callin' Baton Rouge," and he performed that song on the 1994 VH-1 awards with New Grassers Sam Bush and Herb Pedersen, among others.

Dan Hays, executive director of the International Bluegrass Music Association, pointed out that Bob Dylan was recording with Ralph Stanley, who released a CD, *Clinch Mountain Country* by Ralph Stanley and friends. Ricky Skaggs released his first all-bluegrass album in more than a dozen years, *Bluegrass Rules!* (Both albums received Grammy nominations.) Skaggs said that before Bill Monroe died, he'd been concerned that no one would remember him or his music. "I told him, 'There are a lot of people out there who love this music—Vince, Travis Tritt, Joe Diffie,' " Skaggs said. "So we're not going to let it die."

> "Bluegrass music will feel good in this town. I plan to make Guthrie, Oklahoma, the bluegrass capital of the world."
>
> —BYRON BERLINE

Byron Berline and his wife, Bette, had moved back to Bette's hometown of Guthrie, Oklahoma, the town that was the territorial capital of Oklahoma until 1910. Berline had inherited his father's fiddle collection and opened the Double Stop Fiddle Shop in one of Guthrie's historic buildings. A place where fiddles can be bought, traded, and repaired, the shop contains an excellent concert hall where great bluegrass is the order of the day. Every Friday and Saturday night the 170 folding chairs are filled with lucky fans who hear the Byron Berline Band play bluegrass and plenty of other music ranging from western swing to hits by the Beatles. Berline loves it. "I enjoy playing and performing," he said. "I like to see people happy." It was nicer to play to a smaller crowd, he said. "It's better when you can see their faces."

Since leaving Oklahoma, Berline had lent his inimitable fiddle playing to albums by rock and pop legends like Bob Dylan, Elton John, and Mick Jagger, and recorded six solo albums including *Fiddle & a Song*, which was nominated for two Grammy awards. The disc featured guest performances by Vince Gill, Mason Williams, Earl Scruggs, and Bill Monroe.

For years, Berline had been working to bring a bluegrass festival to Guthrie. By October 1997, that dream came true. Oklahoma's International Bluegrass Festival featured top bluegrass performers from the United States and from as far away as Japan, Italy, Austria, Germany, the United Kingdom, and the Czech Republic. The musicians and festival attendees marveled at the beauty of Guthrie, the town with the largest urban district—four hundred blocks—listed on the National Register of Historic Places. Stunning gardens and stained-glass windows grace many of the town's thirteen hundred Victorian cottages. No wonder Guthrie has been called the Bed and Breakfast Capital of Oklahoma. But Guthrie has a somewhat checkered history. The Oklahoma Territory was a haven for outlaws back when there wasn't a federal judge closer than Arkansas or Kansas. The famed Dalton gang hung out in the caves along the Cimarron River, in places with names like Horsethief Canyon. The area was notorious enough to attract famed Hudson River writer Washington Irving, who traveled through the territory writing *A Tour on the Prairies*.

On six stages all over Guthrie, bluegrass music was played and celebrated for three days in October. Many of the smaller acts played at the Preservation Playhouse. The Scottish Rite Temple, a beautiful old auditorium, rang with the sounds of perfectly tuned harmonies and the amazing instrumental work that defines bluegrass. It took the big ballpark, however, to accommodate the crowds that came to see Vince Gill and Ricky Skaggs. The Whites, the Dillards, and other legendary bluegrass musicians like Jim and Jesse showed Guthrie, Oklahoma—and the world—that bluegrass will never die.

> "I got out of high school and my only goal was to make a living playing music. It's kind of gone full circle. I know I'm a country artist, but I got my start in bluegrass music and it will always be very near and dear to me."
>
> —VINCE GILL

The guests assembled at the National Cowboy Hall of Fame in Oklahoma City for the evening's black tie gala were excited as they waited for the guest of honor to arrive. They gathered in the soaring lobby of the building that houses the art, historical memorabilia, and living record of the American West and the people who made it great.

The Visions of the West Donor Recognition Gala on November 25, 1997, took place farther down the long hall in the twelve-hundred-seat Sam Noble Special Events Center, a long room dramatically presided over by six triptych panoramas of the American West by Wilson Hurley. The reception began at 6:30.

Up on the stage, the Oklahoma City Philharmonic Orchestra began to play "Go Rest High on That Mountain," and the city's proudest native son, Vince Gill, sang his most personal and passionate song as the audience sat in utter silence. He followed it with "I Still Believe in You."

Vince, along with Reba McEntire and many others, in-
cluding Gene Autry and "Gunsmoke" actress Amanda
Blake, are among the founding benefactors and capital
campaign donors who supported the creation of the Sam
Noble Special Events Center at the Cowboy Hall of Fame.
This evening, Vince was presented the Hall's bronze
"Wrangler" sculpture in recognition of all his achieve-
ments as an Oklahoman.

Vince's mother, Jerene Gill, was no doubt bursting with
pride at the honor her son received. It had to be a bitter-
sweet moment for Vince. It was just four months after his
father's death.

After Stan Gill died in July 1997, Vince had canceled
several concerts. Later in the year he took some time off to
deal with the emotional turmoil of losing his dad and
facing a divorce. "I've obviously had a really horrible personal life in the past year," he said. "I'm going to watch
my daughter cheerlead at some games. There's a whole lot
of stuff I need to figure out."

The time off gave Vince a chance to see where he
wanted to go next with his music. He said that after *High
Lonesome Sound*, he wanted to make a truly country
album and to try and write more songs by himself. He did
just that over the next nine months. He also spent a lot of
time trying out his new material while playing an amazing
forty-two shows at the Grand Ole Opry.

The Opry audience, both within the theater and over the
radio, was thrilled with the new music. Not only was it
pure, high-quality, brand-new Vince Gill, it was also some
of the most traditional, old-time country music to come
out of late 1990s Nashville. One evening, when Vince was
performing at the Opry, he had a lengthy break between

sets, so he went to his dressing room. He picked up his guitar and started playing. The members of his band joined in. They had a jam session for about an hour, and a crowd of admirers watched for the duration. Everyone in his band took a solo.

On another night at the Opry, in October 1997, Vince took some of his time during the televised segment on TNN to pay tribute to John Denver, who had just died in a plane crash. Vince recalled that he and his father made a home recording of Denver's "Take Me Home, Country Road" when Vince was in junior high school. Vince and John Denver had been golfing buddies and Denver had made a recording of "Jenny Dreamed of Trains" shortly before his death. "Let's honor ole John tonight," Vince said.

Vince Gill learned something about himself during his time off the road.

"I don't want to slow down," he said. "The truth of the matter is that this business tells you when you're done. You don't get to decide. So I'm just having fun while it's still going."

For Vince Gill, there were sad events that gave him the time to really work on *The Key*. In life, sad events are often balanced by some kind of reward for going through them. In this case, the flip side of the sadness was the ability to make this album exactly as he wanted to.

"I've got a lot of pride in the amount of care and time and effort we took to make this record," he said. It was the first time he and his musicians and vocalists were able to cut a lot of different songs and then have so many to choose from for the thirteen that made the final album. "It was fun to take my time and not have to record them all in one sitting. It really made a difference to treasure it a little bit."

What was it that made him want to create and record music that was so much like good old-fashioned country?

"I just missed it," he said. "For a long time, nobody wanted to hear a steel guitar because it defined a song as country. It kind of got to a point where nobody played those crying, really weepy, kind of solos."

Vince had grown up listening to the country music of the fifties and sixties. He didn't have to go looking for those old songs for inspiration while writing the songs for *The Key* because they were all a part of his life, logged into his brain. The album is rooted in his memories. It evokes the things he learned as a child.

> "What was really a joy about making this record is knowing that I didn't want to do any song with a rock groove or a pop groove. I wanted to make a record that was as country at the start as it was at the end."
>
> —VINCE GILL

From the first song on *The Key*, you know that Vince accomplished what he'd set out to do. It's called "Don't Come Cryin' to Me," and he wrote it with Reed Nielsen. It's one of only three songs on the album that Vince wrote with another songwriter. He wrote all the others himself. "Don't Come Cryin' to Me" opens with a great fiddle introduction and immediately showcases a second harmony by Dawn Sears. There's lots of pedal steel and it's traditional all the way, evocative of the best of 1960s country music straight out of Music City. The piano playing is reminiscent of classic country piano stylist Floyd Cramer.

Inspired by the tunes of one of Vince Gill's heroes, Buck Owens, who pioneered the Bakersfield sound in country music, "I Never Really Knew You" has a Saturday-night-at-the-honky-tonk feel that makes you want to get up and take a turn on the floor. This foot-tapper is made even more fun by the background vocals of Sara Evans. In fact, Vince was inspired to invite Sara Evans to sing on the song after he heard her version of the Buck Owens hit "I've Got a Tiger by the Tail."

Soon, though, you quiet down for the next great tune, "Kindly Keep It Country," a slow ballad that pays homage to one of country's greatest crooners, George Jones. It's the second single from *The Key*. With his usual wry sense of humor, Vince said about the song, "It will make Alan Jackson sound like Madonna, it's so country." Acclaimed country newcomer Lee Ann Womack, another country traditionalist, sings a superb harmony that blends beautifully with Vince's voice. "Kindly Keep It Country" is followed by another ballad that harks back to the bluegrass sounds of Kentucky. "All Those Years" is perhaps Vince's way of remembering his early years as a bluegrass singer and picker. Liana Manis and Curtis Young provide the background vocals.

For an Oklahoma native like Vince Gill, Texas is only one state away and one with a similar state of mind. "I'll Take Texas," with background vocals by Shelby Lynne, a singer well known in Nashville circles, is a courteous tip of the Stetson to western swing master Bob Wills and His Texas Playboys and to the artist who's done the most to keep Wills's tradition alive—George Strait. It's a look back at the more innocent times of both life and the music business.

One of the most haunting songs on an album full of potential number-one favorites is "My Kind of Woman/My Kind of Man," a duet with Patty Loveless. The recording sounds as if you're sitting in a holler in Kentucky, listening to the singers perform in the valley below you, filling the air with a rich, pure sound. Patty Loveless once again demonstrates that she has the kind of natural singing voice that can never be learned—you either have it or you don't. The voice itself says as much as the lyrics do. It's an instrument all its own with its own wordless communication.

Vince says he knew he wanted to do a duet with Patty so he was able to write the song with that in mind, tailoring the song to their particular voices, in the perfect key for Patty and himself. "There's a lot of duets that are not written as duets and you have to make key changes to make verses work," he said. "This way it's all in the same key and the melody is structured. It was a blast." Vince Gill and Patty Loveless are two musicians who know one another's strengths well enough to make their voices intertwine and soar. They are truly inside the song in the way that great singers can take you inside, to evoke feelings and make the subject of the lyrics ring true. No wonder it received a Grammy nomination for Country Collaboration with Vocals.

"There's Not Much Love Here Anymore," written solely by Vince Gill, features background vocals by Shelby Lynne. Vince sings this with an incredible amount of feeling and the authority of someone who's been there. It's a reminder of a late sixties–early seventies Nashville production, featuring an interplay between the strings and the pedal steel guitar.

"Let Her In" is the story of a man who wants his child to accept a new woman in his life. Vince said he was inspired to write this song by the experience of a friend. It's an up-tempo tune that belies the seriousness of the subject.

Only Vince Gill, country's poet of hearts, can tackle a subject and convey in just a few verses and choruses the essence of a deep emotional situation in such a clearly understood way. The harmonies, acoustic guitars, and pedal steel show echoes of Pure Prairie League. Here Vince has taken an old song structure and made it new. Jeff White, Billy Thomas, and Sonya Isaacs sing background vocals.

Alison Krauss joins Jeff White, Billy Thomas, and Vince on background vocals for "The Hills of Caroline." Another solo songwriting achievement for Vince, it's a three-minute movie—the listener is compelled by the lyrics and the music track to visualize the story. A boy grows up, becomes a man, learns about love from a special woman, and then laments her loss—"she's gone to live with Jesus." He asks at the end of his life to be buried next to her, all in the hills of Carolina. In this beautiful song, shimmering with the sounds of the mandolin and fiddle, Vince Gill's bluegrass roots are evident. It is also a testament to his songwriting talent—the song could easily have been written forty years ago but is in fact brand-new. "The Hills of Caroline" is as close to pure Appalachian folk music as anyone can get, as authentic an American folk song as anything written by Woody Guthrie or Bill Monroe.

Vince wrote "Live to Tell It All" with Sonya Isaacs, a member of the Isaacs family gospel group, whose voice harmonizes with his on the song. "She's just one of those artists with a pure voice. Her pitch is incredible, just one of those angelic voices." The song promises truly unconditional love, love that will be there even if things go bad, played in a most traditional country style. A great guitar solo again demonstrates that Vince's guitar solos don't simply fill space, they have a voice just as lyrical as the vocal.

The lovely and talented Faith Hill, whose star has been rising high in recent years with songs like "This Kiss" and duets with her husband, Tim McGraw, joins Vince on "What They All Call Love."

Vince returned the favor, singing with her on "Let Me Let Go," the second number-one hit single from her latest album, *Faith.*

The contributions of the musicians are as perfectly rendered as those of the vocalists on *The Key.* For this album, Vince and producer Tony Brown hired some very traditional country players to join the major Nashville session players whose talents are on display here. There's Hargus "Pig" Robbins, who's played on hundreds of records, from Patsy Cline's to Bob Dylan's. Steve Gibson has also played for numerous music stars and played in actor/ singer Jerry Reed's hit-making band. Randy Scruggs, son of bluegrass master Earl Scruggs, and a great musician in his own right, plays acoustic piano. These are just a few of the many top-notch studio musicians on *The Key*, players who are veterans of countless albums who look forward to playing with Vince Gill because they know he is an equal as a musician and whose own talents push them to achieve their best.

> "Every note counts on these records and every person's contribution counts. It's a combination of people's hearts, souls, and sounds."
>   —VINCE GILL

The critical acclaim for *The Key* was unanimous. One major newspaper said Vince Gill was approaching country

legend Hank Williams Sr. in expressing the depths of love
gone wrong and compared the album's lyrics to those of
pop icon James Taylor. Mario Tarradell in the *Dallas
Morning News* called the album "his most cohesive work
to date. Mr. Gill's signature sound—the crystalline choruses, the crisp melodies—remains intact as he shuffles
through rich country hallmarks." *People* magazine said,
"This all-around splendid country album is testimony to
Gill's ascension. Vince Gill discovers the key to success:
winning songs, beautifully sung." *Los Angeles Times* pop
critic Robert Hilburn said of "If You Ever Have Forever
in Mind": "Gill's showstopping vocal on this heartache
ballad rivals not merely anything by such country greats as
George Jones but also the soulful grace of such country-
influenced r&b singers such as Ray Charles and Otis Red-
ding." The song received two Grammy nominations—Male
Country Vocal Performance and Country Song of the Year.

USA Today called *The Key* "as purely traditional a
country album as anyone has released this year." Yet as
country as it was, *The Key* also charted high on *Billboard*'s
pop albums chart.

At Fan Fair in June 1998, Vince Gill and Jenny Gill co-
hosted the Tuesday evening MCA Records Show on a
stage in the Nashville Motor Speedway, right on the Tennessee State Fair Grounds in Nashville.

Jenny Gill had been playing with a few different bands
in many of the coffeehouses in Nashville where all kinds
of music can be heard. "She doesn't have any idea how
neat it feels to me to watch her up there doing what she
does," Vince said. At some of his own shows in 1997,
Vince had invited Jenny to sing with him and the audiences had loved hearing dad and daughter on such songs

as Shania Twain's "You're Still the One" or Deana Carter's "Strawberry Wine." "She walks out there," Vince said, "and I might as well not be playing because I'm just Dad holding a guitar."

Many of those sitting in the audience at the MCA show were delighted to see Vince's daughter on stage with him. They had already met him in the big booth set up by CMT, Country Music Television, the music video network that was sponsoring his 1998 tour. The personal warmth and truly good-heartedness of Vince Gill came through, as always, as he greeted and thanked his fans. Hearing him team up with Olivia Newton-John to sing the John Travolta part in the song "The One That I Want" from the hit movie *Grease* only confirmed to these loyal fans that when it comes to music, this man can do just about anything.

> "I'm glad to be back out on tour. I haven't been out in nine months. . . . I've forgotten how to play guitar."
>
> —VINCE GILL

Well, he hadn't forgotten at all. He did say, "I haven't played much but I can beat just about anybody in golf, with all that time off."

The thousands and thousands of concertgoers who saw Vince Gill in 1998 in the CMT-sponsored tour that took him to fifty cities coast to coast were treated to some of the best guitar-playing around.

"We're just gonna go out there and play it loud," he said. "I remember when I didn't have any hits. Now, if I played everything, we'd be there eight hours."

Maybe he didn't play eight hours on stage, but Vince did get to play almost all day before the shows. His sound checks are longer than some artists' concerts! At each concert location, all the instruments and sound equipment are set up early in the day and the location's own sound system is activated. Engineers work hard to make sure that the music the fans hear will sound as good as it can. Since each venue is different, the sound check can never be skipped.

Vince wouldn't want to, anyway. He loves sound checks. Often the band doesn't even play the songs in the show. "We just go and start jamming," Vince says. "We're not trying to get it done as quickly as we can and then go hang out and do nothing again. We like to play." The road crew calls Vince and his band "Grateful Gill," likening them to the marathon-length Grateful Dead concerts millions have enjoyed. "We don't practice our dance moves or anything," Vince adds. "We just play music."

Vince is so relaxed before his shows that journalists who've interviewed dozens of high-strung performers are usually amazed. He doesn't go through a lot of pre-concert routines and rituals. He just changes his shirt and heads for the stage. "I think sometimes people take their success and their career and their whole deal too seriously," he says. "I really don't. . . . I just try to be normal."

Opening acts for Vince in the summer of 1998 included rising star Chely Wright, the newly reunited group Restless Heart, and his longtime friend and tourmate Patty Loveless.

How's this for a sort of dream come true in reverse? One night, Patty's guitar player had to rush home because his wife went into labor. So Vince sat in. "I got to play with Patty all weekend being her guitar player," he said. "It was more fun than I had all year long because I got to go up there and just be a musician and play with the band. My adrenaline was going through the roof." Afterward, he went out and played his own full set. He was like the bride who isn't supposed to be seen in her dress before the wedding, but he didn't care.

Many of the shows were outdoors—at state and county fairs, in big stadiums and arenas. "Bugs in your teeth, hundred-degree heat, oh it's a lot of fun," Vince said. "No, but I'm serious, it really is good fun."

Each show is different, a great mix of ballads and loose, up-tempo material with plenty of jamming to show off the great band. Vince isn't as strict as some artists about keeping the songs exact replicas of the recordings. He also doesn't have the big productions—the laser lights, explosive smoke, and special effects—other stars have. "I'm not criticizing the acts who have big productions," Vince says. "I think their shows are awesome, but that's not me. I don't do any tricks. I just like to play the music." Vince says when he goes to concerts, he wants to hear them more than see them.

> "I love to play; I've waited my whole life to get
> to play as much as I wanted."
>
> —VINCE GILL

Some musicians arrive at a show asking, "How long do I have to play?" Vince Gill would ask, "How long do I get to play?" For as long as the fans wanted him, he'd stay on-stage, stretching out his own lead guitar solos, giving plenty of time to his band members to show off their stuff, and showing the fans that a guy who loves what he does can keep doing it all night.

"Buyers and promoters love Vince," says Rick Shipp, head of the Nashville office of the William Morris Agency, "because he's one of the few acts in this genre that can pull off a two-hour-plus show and still leave the audience wanting more."

For years he'd been the opening act, always told he could only play a thirty- or forty-five-minute set. "Now I'm out there having a big time and I've recorded a lot of songs and I like singing them. I don't look at playing live as, you know, 'Go sing a handful of hit songs, collect the check and get back on the bus.' I love getting to play."

At the New York State Fair in Syracuse, New York, in August, Vince bantered with the audience. When he introduced "What the Cowgirls Do" by saying, "I'd sure like to know what the Syracuse cowgirls do," all the cowgirls in the audience were up on their feet to show him. Later in that concert, he said, "There's a man out there with a sign that says, 'If you kiss my woman, I might get lucky tonight.' I'm here to tell you, son, if I kiss her, I might get lucky." The fans loved it.

"It's really neat that country music has such a broad demographic," Vince Gill says, "and it's not just for one generation of people anymore. I'm pretty lucky because I have a pretty full scope of ages who come to my show." He thinks one reason the older folks like him is "because I have a gentleman's haircut" and that the kids like him "because I play the guitar loud and they have a good time."

Everyone in the audience seems to loved the long guitar solos. Vince has said he worries that some fans don't want to hear all that guitar playing, that they've come to his shows to hear him sing. Under the stars in Syracuse, the fans of all ages were sitting in amazement as the ten flying fingers of Vincent Grant Gill played about ten different guitars. For some, his exceptional picking was a surprise.

"Maybe people don't think of me as a player because I don't make it look hard," Vince says.

> "I'm thinking of writing a guitar instruction book that is all made up of facial expressions that make it look like what you're doing is really hard."
>
> —VINCE GILL

Breath of Heaven, Vince Gill's second collection of Christmas songs, was released in October 1998. From the first notes of "Winter Wonderland," we see again one reason why Vince is such a great talent. It's phrasing—that unique way of putting the words of a song together, drawing one out, skimming over another. It's why even in singing the most familiar songs, he can put a new sound to them.

"Chestnuts roasting on an open fire"—the lyrics everyone knows from the Mel Torme/Robert Wells "The Christmas Song" come through the speakers and astonish us anew in Vince's voice. A great selection of classic Christmas carols gets the Vince Gill treatment. Accompanying him is Patrick Williams and His Orchestra. Tony Brown and Patrick Williams produced the album, which garnered two Grammy nominations.

The title song, "Breath of Heaven (Mary's Song),"

written by Amy Grant and Chris Eaton, is a universal song of the love we celebrate at Christmas. Vince does it beautifully.

The album was recorded in the old Capitol Studios in Hollywood where Frank Sinatra, Bing Crosby, and Nat King Cole made their classic records. The sound and arrangements on "Breath of Heaven" bring Vince far from country and into the realm of the singers who recorded at Capitol Studios before him. Not content to just make another album to fill the racks at Christmas, Vince Gill took the opportunity to stretch his talents in yet another direction. The sound of the album is pure, beautiful music sung by one of the greatest voices of any genre or any time. The album hit the Top 10 country albums chart and will likely be a seasonal favorite for years to come.

At the 1998 Country Music Association Awards, nationally televised on CBS on September 23, Vince Gill did his usual excellent job, helping the show win its time slot in the ratings. Dressed in a gorgeous black tuxedo, he started the show by playing a guitar duet with Randy Scruggs. As the names of all the performers and presenters were announced, Vince and Randy regaled the audience with a great rendition of "Soldier's Joy," a song from Scruggs's new album, which received a Grammy nomination.

Later in the show, Vince, who has won more CMA awards than any other artist in the history of the organization, showed his colleagues and fans how at home he felt with them all. Accompanied only by his own acoustic guitar playing, he sang "The Key to Life."

"This is the first guitar I ever saw in my life," he said,

"and it was my daddy's. He taught me two or three chords on this thing, and this is how I remember it."

Even after performing the song countless times on his major coast-to-coast tour the previous summer, it was here among his friends in the hallowed hall of the Grand Ole Opry that Vince seemed most emotional in playing and singing "The Key." He choked up several times. But his guitar playing rang sweet and true and the audience began to applaud even before he finished.

Family matters a great deal to Vince Gill. He is devoted to his daughter, Jenny, now seventeen years old. And not surprisingly, Jenny has some musical talents of her own. "I love to sing harmony anyway," Vince said, "but I was really amazed at what it was like to sing with my own blood." Growing up, he used to sing at home with his father. He even got his father on stage once to sing with him, an experience he loved. "And now to be able to do that with my daughter, I felt that whole blood thing."

When Jenny became old enough to drive, Vince joked that he hadn't seen her since she'd gotten her own car!

Talk about not slowing down, Vince Gill was as busy as always. He could be heard on the *Tribute to Tradition* album on which Sony Records asked artists to perform an old song that influenced their music.

Vince played on his friend Randy Scruggs's new album, *Crown of Jewels*, along with Randy's father, Earl. He was also asked by Sonya Isaacs to produce her solo album and was thrilled to say yes. When the Grand Ole Opry played its first show at the Ryman Auditorium in twenty-five years, Vince Gill was the first star to say he'd be there. And when "Whisperin' Bill" Anderson released his first new album in seventeen years, he said his collaboration with Vince Gill on "Which Bridge to Cross (Which Bridge to Burn)" had helped make it possible.

> "I look at things in a very realistic way. With my family, everything had to make sense. I have good sense about what's going to happen."
>   —VINCE GILL

The kid who left home at eighteen hoping to be able to pay his rent while working as a musician had made that, and so much more, happen for himself. "I feel lucky that I've achieved what I've achieved and gotten to do what I've gotten to do—maybe even more so in the years that were lean, in the years I didn't have hits," Vince said. "There were several places where the band outnumbered the audience."

But he didn't give up. Somehow he must have known that success was going to come eventually. "I had seven years to sit there and watch everybody else win, being involved with it but kind of on the outskirts," he said. "Now I've been a big part of it for seven years and if it keeps coming, it'll surprise me. I certainly don't want it to go away, but I know it will."

Even if it does go away, Vince Gill will always be an icon, a symbol not only of country music in the 1990s but of pop in the 1980s and bluegrass in the 1970s. His achievement is that he has taken all of those categories and made another one—excellent music that transcends them all. It's more than likely that when people name the great singers of the twentieth century, Vince Gill will be on the list. His guitar-playing will always be regarded as among the best there is. And the songs he's written are already classics that will live on as long as anyone appreciates good music.

In a 1998 year-end report on the state of country music, Vince Gill was listed as one of the mainstays of country radio. Years ago, he'd hoped to gain that level of respect. Now he has exceeded his expectations.

The best part about being Vince Gill the star is that he doesn't define himself by it. Even if he loses his spot at the top of the country music mountain, he'll never lose his love of playing and making wonderful music. He's still a man with Oklahoma values, the common sense to know that all the popularity and record sales are temporary, the character to know what really counts in life.

"I'm not afraid of when they're going to go, 'Click! Next!' Because it's going to happen," he says. "To deny that it's going to happen is foolish. Maybe I'll be one of the lucky ones, like George Strait, who has real longevity. And I think that's because I haven't always tried to make a record that fit the mold for that week. I've tried to consistently record good songs. The good songs will always win."

He's right. From the start, Vince Gill did everything for the music. It might have taken a while, but the music ultimately did everything for him.

"I love what I'm doing. If I stop having hits—which I will at some point, I'm sure—I'm not going to quit doing it," he says. "I'm still going to record, and I'm going to travel some, play the Opry a bunch, play a lot of golf, and just live my life."

But for now? "There's nothing better than doing what you love and having people appreciate it."

Vince Gill's Albums

QUADRUPLE PLATINUM
I Still Believe in You

DOUBLE PLATINUM
When I Call Your Name
Pocket Full of Gold
When Love Finds You

PLATINUM
Souvenirs
Let There Be Peace on Earth
High Lonesome Sound

GOLD
The Best of Vince Gill
I Never Knew Lonely

SOON TO BE PLATINUM
The Key
Breath of Heaven

Acknowledgments

I have met and talked with a lot of people about music in my career as a journalist and as an author of four country music biographies. But I have never found the range of knowledge, depth of understanding, intelligent insight, and sheer savvy possessed by my husband, Ira Fraitag. I'm not the only one who feels this way, as any number of other professionals in the music business will attest. Ira's contributions to *For the Music* are huge and were given with his characteristic generosity and love.

All the folks at Ballantine Books did their usual great job. I would like to particularly thank Betsy Flagler for her smart editing, sharp eye for photos, and unflagging support.

Lauren Bufferd and all the folks at the Country Music Foundation Library in Nashville were once again tremendously kind and helpful in the research for this book. Robin Davison at the *Daily Oklahoman* graciously welcomed me into the newspaper's impressive offices. I'd like to thank Robin and all the wonderful people of Oklahoma City for being some of the best folks on earth.

My three pals at Entertainment Management Group—the ever-amusing Sol Saffian, the spirited Jerry Cohen, and Ira Fraitag—all know how to make work fun without sacrificing one bit of professionalism.

Special thanks to Josh Laroff for research assistance and to Harold Laroff for his constant enthusiasm for my books. Ali Sgammato has also contributed greatly to the marketing of my titles, and for that, I thank her.

I was a fan of Vince Gill's before I stated writing this book, and I am even more of a fan now. Researching and learning all about him by reading everything ever written about him, journeying to Oklahoma City and Norman, Oklahoma, and listening dozens of times to all of his amazing songs made me feel very close to him even though I didn't interview him directly. I have been singing his praises for months, and I expect to do so for years to come.

I'd also like to thank all of my family and friends, who bring so much joy into my life.

DREAM COME TRUE
The LeAnn Rimes Story
by Jo Sgammato

LeAnn Rimes, owner of a huge, God-given voice, was born knowing what she wanted to do and sang with assurance when she was just a toddler. Here is the heartwarming story of LeAnn Rimes and her parents, Belinda and Wilbur Rimes, an American family who made a DREAM COME TRUE.

COUNTRY'S GREATEST DUO
The Brooks & Dunn Story
by Jo Sgammato

Just mention foot-stomping honky tonk tunes, rich ballads, stylish videos, and an awesome stage show and people know you're talking about Brooks & Dunn. The Country Music Association's Duo of the Year for six years running—and the only pair to win the coveted Entertainer of the Year Award—Brooks & Dunn have created a rockin' country sound all their own.

TOE TAPPIN' TRIVIA
BRET NICHOLAUS AND PAUL LOWRIE
The Country Music Book that Gets You Singin' and Keeps You Guessin'

• In Garth Brooks's "Much Too Young (to Feel this Damn Old)," his debut top-ten hit, the main character mentions that he has a worn-out tape of which male country singer?

• Willie Nelson and Waylon Jennings had a huge hit with their duet "Mammas Don't Let Your Babies Grow Up to Be Cowboys." After warning mothers not to let their babies become cowboys, what professions do they encourage mammas to let their babies pursue?

• In Alabama's classic "Mountain Music," the main character says that they'll float on down the river in order to get to what?

The bestselling authors of *The Conversation Piece* have combed the country for lyrical nuggets that will have you matching wits with friends and family in a tuneful trivia tribute.